For as long  e earth there have been stories. The practice of storytelling is more than just an act of communication: It is an aspect of human nature and has been integral to every culture throughout history. Before the written word there were storytellers. In towns, villages, and camps people would circle the storyteller to listen to what was being shared. These storytellers told their stories for many reasons: To pass knowledge, to explain natural events, to chronicle history, and sometimes just to entertain.

I was hired in July of 2000 as a recruit for the Police Department in Omaha, Nebraska. I was forced to end my career eleven years later due to Post Traumatic Stress Disorder stemming from events "on the job." During my career I was honored to work with a very wise Patrol Sergeant who believed that his crew and select others needed a place to occasionally meet and tell the stories of the day in order to decompress and keep life in perspective. That place was in fact a circle at the end of an unused street way out by the airport. The "88" comes from the police radio code used to describe the "Situation Secure;"

Hence the name of this book. Many a story was told at that circle, and that circle will always hold a special place in my heart.

This book is a collection of my stories. All are true and I have attempted to relate them as accurately as possible without embellishment. As a final note, I decided to keep the other actors in this book as anonymous as possible due to the fact that many are still on the job.

I hope you the reader enjoy reading these stories as much as I enjoyed living them.

CHAPTERS:

"HE CAME AND HE WENT"

"SORRY KID, THAT'S MY CRUISER"

"NOT ALWAYS SAFE IN YOUR HOLE"

"A ROOKIE JUST GOT BOMBED"

"LETTUCE CRISPER LATRINE"

"A CAR FULL OF GUNS"

"RUN TURKEYS, RUN!"

"BODYWORK LESSON"

"SUCKER WITH AN EXTRA BADGE"

"IT'S TOO LATE TO GIVE UP NOW"

"THAT NICKNAME WILL STICK"

"CHOW-CHOW PART TWO"

"I'M MISSING SOME CUFFS, AND A SUSPECT"

"DUDE, YOU ARE SLOW"

"PROPHETIC COFFEE CUP"

"PARKING WOULD HAVE BEEN SMARTER"

"AGAINST ALL ODDS GUN CATCH"

"DIDN'T SEE THAT COMING"

"GO AHEAD AND TAKE A PISS"

"THAT'S WHY THEY'RE NUMBERED"

"DON'T BRING A SHOVEL TO A TASER FIGHT"

"THE SHOES DIDN'T MOVE"

"NEW YEAR'S AT HANK'S PLACE"

"ANOTHER NEW YEAR'S"

"GONNA NEED A SCALP SURGEON"

"RETIRE THAT CRUISER"

"DOORS DON'T WORK LIKE THAT"

"CRACK SPIT-WAD"

"FIREMAN TEN-COUNT"

"SCARED TO THE GROUND BY THE SOUND"

"GET SOME WOOD"

"THAT'S HOW YOU CARRY A LITTLE FELON"

"WABBIT SEASON"

"FOOT CHASE…CHASE"

"LISTEN TO YOUR MOMMA"

"WORST CALL EVER"

"CRACK WAVE"

"TAKE THAT CHAMP"

"SERIOUS HANDCUFFING VIOLATION"

"THE STEAMING GUN"

"CARROTS IN THE DRESSER"

"LISTEN, I'VE GOT WEED"

"TRASH CAN SKS"

"THANK GOD FOR THE SECOND CRUISER"

"17 ROUND MIRACLE"

"THAT'S NOT PANCAKE MIX"

"4TH OF JULY FAMILY BONDING"

"VIDEO FOOTAGE OF HIS FAVORITE COP"

"BLIZZARD BURGLAR"

"TOO MUCH PEPPER"

"DIRECTIONS FROM A CONCERNED CITIZEN"

"WHO KNEW SPIDERS LIKE CRACK"

"2CX BODY REPAIR"

"THROWING AWAY THE CAR KEYS"

"C.C.W. TRIFECTA"

"PROFESSIONAL INSTALL"

"I FELL ON THE GUN"

"ONE GUN GOOD, TWO GUNS BETTER"

"C.C.W. SELFIE"

"NICE SHOOTING, YOU GOT'EM BOTH"

"LESS IS MORE"

"ROLL YOUR WINDOWS UP WHEN IGNORING DIRECTIONS"

"DIRECT LINE"

"IF I'M THE FIFTH, THERE WON'T BE A SIXTH"

"CRUISER STRIP SEARCH BLUFF"

"NICE DOG BARK"

"AIRPORT D.U.I."

"WALKING THE DEUCE STRAPPED"

"THE DEUCE CONTINUED"

"DON'T THROW COCKED REVOLVERS"

"PREP THE ROOM FOR THE FIGHT"

"MY SPECIAL UNDERWEAR"

"EASTER EGG GUN HUNT"

"HOUSE PARTY GUNS"

"JUMPED WITH THE FAMILY"

"UNWELCOMED CHIROPRACTIC SERVICES"

"ONE-GLOVE, THANKS MEDIA"

"38 MINUTE PURSUIT, BUY A KIA"

"THE RULES OF INTERNAL AFFAIRS"

"THE SPHINC-TE-LATOR"

"ONLY DOGS AND DOLPHINS HEARD THAT"

"GUNS IN THE GRASS"

"THANKS FIRE MARSHALL"

"PAY PHONE CRACK DISPENSER"

"EXCALIBUR FOOT CHASE"

"NEVER LOAN YOUR PHONE"

"JUST WAITING PATIENTLY"

"CAREER ENDER"

"HE CAME AND HE WENT"

This story is first in the book because it's one of the earliest memories from my career. I had just finished field training and was out on my own, working my first crew. It felt good to finally be a "real cop" without a coach looking over my shoulder. The purpose of field training with coaches is obvious—to expose the recruits to what day to day life as a cop really entails. Well, that's great on paper, but the time spent in field training doesn't prepare you for everything. Not even close.

The crew had just finished roll-call and everyone was loading up their cruisers. As usual, the veterans were taking their time, and the rookies were hurrying to get on the radio to inform dispatch they were ready for calls. There's a reason the veterans don't hurry. When 911 calls come in during shift change the dispatchers hold the non-priority report calls for the on-coming shift. On this day I was the first car from the northwest precinct to hit into service. Immediately I was dispatched to the first call— "Make an Investigation." Here's what that dispatch really means: There's a dead body waiting for you when you get to your address.

This was one of those calls I never handled during field training. Right away my heart started racing because I had no clue what to do. Lucky for me, the crustiest veteran cop on the crew heard the dispatch and hit me up via car-to-car communication and volunteered to go with me. Relieved I started off towards my destination. Somehow the vet beat me to the address and was waiting outside his car with Vick's, a cigar, and a strange smile. He could see the curiosity on my face and explained what he was holding before I could ask.

The explanation is simple: The dispatcher doesn't tell you how long the person has been dead, so best to be prepared for a bad smell. Now that I had been enlightened it was time for the inevitable entry into the house. We were met by a friend of the family that had discovered the deceased. Fortunately, the time of death was recent so there was no need to light the cigars and stick Vick's up our noses. It was time to start the investigation. The reporting party directed us into the bedroom where the departed was found. It got weird real quick.

For starters, the guy, who looked to be about fifty-five, was naked lying on his side on the bed.

He was facing a T.V. that was sitting on a stand not far away. After taking some time to assess the room and what could be observed of the body without touching it, the vet and I both agreed it didn't look like foul play. Here's how we arrived at that conclusion: This took place back in the time of VCR's. What we, and the now deceased were watching on the television throughout the investigation was hardcore porn. We surmised the VCR had an auto-play feature that kept restarting the VHS tape every time it got to the end. After careful examination of the body we noted that one hand on the dead guy was frozen in place in his groin region.

It didn't take any sort of specialized training to formulate the working theory about what had happened in the room. After calling the Homicide unit and the Coroner I sat down in the living room of the house to make out the initial incident report pending the upcoming autopsy. The vet decided he had seen enough and asked me if I needed any more help. I told him no, and thanked him for taking the call with me. He grinned at me almost deviously and stated as he walked out the front door, "He came and he went." I was shocked and didn't know how to react to his statement. A guy had just died pleasuring himself and I had to find a way to write that into an official police report! It was at that moment I realized—Cops have a warped sense of humor.

SORRY KID, THAT'S MY CRUISER

This is another early story from when I was a rookie Cop making stupid mistakes and bad decisions on a daily basis. There's an old saying that goes something like "God looks out for children and fools." Looking back I think you can add cops to that list. I know for me it played out on many occasions. Here's one of those times.

It was a really hot summer day and I was working the northwest Omaha afternoon shift, referred to as "C" shift. That shift lasts roughly from 3 P.M. to 11 P.M. "A" shift is the overnight shift, and "B" shift is the day shift. "C" shift as a general rule is the busiest and most action packed of the three shifts. As a result, that is where most rookies start their career, since shift is based on seniority. I was fine with that since the "action" is one of the reasons I chose law enforcement.

I was dispatched with a veteran Officer to "check a party." Someone had called 911 to report a teenager in an apartment complex parking lot acting strangely. These are some of the worst calls you can get because they lack details, meaning you are going in blind. This dispatch came right at the beginning of the shift, which in this case makes a huge impact on the outcome of this story. You see, the vet I was dispatched with was a stickler for routines; his own routines. One of his routines dictated he didn't do any police work until he first stopped for coffee. This usually took about the first twenty minutes of his shift.

Since this was a two Officer call, protocol dictates the first arriving Officer waits for the second Officer a safe distance from the call address. Me being the rookie I drove straight there and camped out to wait for the vet who I knew would be forever getting there due to the coffee stop. I had parked close enough to see the parking lot where this teenager was supposed to be, and sure enough he was there. He seemed completely oblivious to the fact that I was watching him, even though I was parked in plain sight in broad daylight. After watching him for a couple of minutes I agreed with whomever had called 911—this kid was acting strange. He was wearing only a pair of cut off jean shorts and pacing around like a caged tiger. Occasionally he would sit down on the curb for an instant, and then he would be back to pacing. I must have watched this go on for ten minutes as I awaited the arrival of my coffee drinking colleague.

Finally I had enough and decided it was time to act without my backup: Mistake number one. I drove my cruiser straight into the middle of the parking lot where this kid was located. I got out of the cruiser, leaving it running, and made my initial approach: Mistake numbers two and three. Now usually when a cop drives up next to a person they at least give some signs of recognition or acknowledgment. Not this kid, he acted like he didn't see me, and maybe he didn't. It was pretty obvious this kid was under the influence of some substance, or substances.

I started talking to this kid and finally he looks at me and starts babbling incoherently. I was trying to ask him a set of rational questions to which I received gibberish in response. The whole time I'm thinking in the back of my mind, geez how long does it take to get coffee? At one point I got the kid to sit on the curb while I was standing next to my open cruiser door: Mistake number four. All of the sudden the kid launches off the curb, runs straight at me, knocks me out of the way, gets behind the wheel of my **RUNNING CRUISER WITH A SHOTGUN IN IT** and closes the door! To say that I was stunned would be the ultimate understatement. Here's the part where God looking out for cops comes into play.

Luckily for me this kid was so high he didn't realize the cruiser was already running. So, he's in there trying to start the running cruiser, grinding the crap out of the starter! The other stroke of luck for me was that I had left the driver's side window down. After quickly realizing the many errors in judgement I composed myself and began to move into action. The first thing I did was to get on the radio as calmly as possible to tell my backup Officer to "step it up!" The second thing I did was to reach inside the open driver's window and put a death grab on the gearshift knob of the Crown Victoria with my left hand. I figured if I had to I would break the gearshift knob off to prevent this kid from driving off. Next, with every ounce of strength and adrenaline I had I started hitting this kid in the face with my right fist in backhand strikes. I can't tell you how many times I hit him, but I can tell you it was totally ineffective. The whole time the kid just kept trying to start the cruiser!

After what felt like forever, the kid just stopped what he was doing and opened the car door like I wasn't there. This was also the same time my partner on this call decided to show up. The kid, totally calm and bleeding from the face pushed past me and went back to sitting on the curb where he was before. My partner saw only the tail end of this and ran over to help me. I was completely out of breath and strength at that point and could barely talk. My partner walked over to the kid stood him up and proceeded to put him in handcuffs without further incident.

After putting the kid in the back of the cruiser I was finally able to describe to my partner what had happened in his absence. Long story short the kid turned out to be sixteen, so we had to take him to the hospital and call his parents. The parents showed up to the hospital and we all found out together that the kid was high on PCP. I of course had to tell the parents what had happened since I had to explain the condition of their son's face. At the end of it all the parents thanked me for not killing their kid, the hospital kept the youngster, and I learned several valuable lessons.

NOT ALWAYS SAFE IN YOUR HOLE

Every six months the Omaha Police Department holds what is called the semi-annual bid board. This is the established process by which assignments are chosen for all those in the Uniform Patrol Bureau. This is of course done by seniority. After my first year they had another academy class graduate so I finally had at least some seniority and wouldn't have to settle for one of the last spots that nobody wanted. I was thrilled. I ended up getting on a crew that was made up predominately of younger Officers from the two classes before mine. This is when I realized how much fun the job could be when you start to feel that sense of camaraderie with your fellow crewmates.

There were twelve people on the crew, and five of us had formed a small clique. We would tend to congregate in out of the way spots, known as "holes" in the downtime between radio calls. A hole is a spot that is hidden from the prying eyes of the public, but yet open enough to prevent someone from approaching without being noticed. Prime examples are parking lots behind closed businesses, city parks after closing, etc. For lots of cops you can almost set your watch by what time of their shift they would "head for the hole." One of the guys in our little clique was like that. He had his hole that he would go to every night by himself to finish his paperwork prior to the end of the shift.

During this six month rotation the Omaha Police Department had just deployed their newest tool in the fight against crime: The pepper-ball gun. These are essentially paintball guns on steroids that fire plastic balls filled with Oleoresin Capsicum, (O.C.). Or put another way, a powder version of the stuff found in mace, or pepper spray. In order to be certified to carry and use these pepperball guns you had to get shot with it first. I can attest it hurts a lot, even when shot with the inert training ammunition. I have another story for that later.

Back to this story, when it comes to Cops they tend to be creatures of habit, like the habit of writing reports in the same hole at the same time every night. Cops also tend to like practical jokes. One particularly slow night our clique got a bright idea towards the end of the shift. Well, it was four of the five of our clique since one was sitting in his hole writing reports. One by one the four of us snuck back to the precinct building and retrieved a pepperball gun from the equipment room, making sure to fill the ammunition hoppers. Then we coordinated the rally point for the meet prior to assaulting our unsuspecting co-worker.

Now when pepperballs are deployed it can be done in two ways: Either by direct fire, or by indirect fire. Direct fire inflicts pain on the target, in addition to the irritation of the chemical. Indirect fire is usually used for crowds by dispersing the chemical into a cloud by exploding the pepperballs against something hard nearby, or by firing into the ground. Our poor co-worker and friend got both.

When we planned the attack we just intended to scare him a little, since he was kind of a nervous guy anyway. Things quickly got out of control as soon as the attack began. We had parked our cruisers nearby and gone in on foot by stealth. Once we were all close enough we could see that our buddy was dutifully completing his reports from the supposed safety of his cruiser. Fortunately for the four of us attacking, the car windows were wide open since it was such a pleasant summer evening. The original plan was to shoot the sides of the cruiser to startle our pal and give him a taste of the pepperball powder. Nobody stuck to the plan. As soon as we started shooting it became clear that none of us was going to stop shooting until our guns were dry.

The first ping against the cruiser had sent pen and paper flying. We could see that plain as day since the dome light was on inside the car. That just fueled our attack. In an instant pepperballs were impacting every square inch of the cruiser, and more than a few of them made it inside the open windows. At least one struck our poor buddy in the side of the neck. When the shooting stopped the cruiser was enveloped in a toxic white cloud of pepper powder. Suffice it to say our buddy was not happy with us. There was the additional problem of what to do with the car, which was now totally polluted. There was no way that cruiser could be turned over to the next shift. So, it got parked with the windows down and some made up excuse about why it couldn't be driven. Fortunately, neither the car nor our buddy suffered any permanent effects.

A ROOKIE JUST GOT BOMBED

When it comes to practical jokes nobody does them better than cops. They're usually harmless like moving a co-worker's cruiser around the corner while they're inside someone's house taking a report. Another favorite is spraying just a little bit of mace down the air ducts by the windshield on a cold day so that when the defroster is turned on it fumigates the inside of the cruiser. Part of what makes pranks so much fun is that it sets the stage for revenge.

When I came on the job Omaha was behind the times when it came to radio equipment. Back in 2000 the radio communications system was still based in analog technology. This meant that the radios and the rest of the emergency equipment in the cruisers were old and very different from today's current digital technology. That being said, there used to be a very popular prank that would inevitably get pulled on every rookie sometime during the field training process. The prank was called the "microphone bomb" or "mic bomb" for short.

Now I don't know who pioneered the "mic bomb" or when the first one happened, but I do know they are fondly remembered by all that ever witnessed one. I'm a little fuzzy on the memory of how to set up a "mic bomb" but I'll do my best to describe the process, and more importantly the end result.

"Mic bombs" were best delivered at Central Headquarters for maximum embarrassment effect. It used to be that the jail was in the basement of the downtown headquarters building. Access to the jail required driving into a secure parking garage underneath the six story building. This garage was ideal for magnifying sound. The prank obviously starts when the recruit or "boot" as they are affectionately referred to, steps out of sight of the car by entering the building. Then the "bomb" had to be set. Here's how it was done.

The light and siren controls had a separate power knob that had to be turned on anytime the system was going to be used. It also had a separate microphone that was used when operating the P.A. system. This microphone was just like the kind you see on cop cars on T.V., a handheld microphone with a button on the side that gets depressed by the thumb to activate it. For this prank, the microphone was wedged between the closed driver's door and the driver's seat bottom. Wedging it between the door and the seat kept the button depressed until the door was opened. The sirens in the old systems were based on a toggle switch that had to be manually operated and turned on separately from everything else. For whatever reason, the sirens would not operate when the microphone button was depressed and the toggle switch was set to one of the three siren modes. That is, until the driver's side car door was opened by the unsuspecting recruit. Once that happened, the sirens would activate and stay on until turned off via the toggle switch. The sound of a police siren in an enclosed garage is deafening.

The true beauty of the "bomb" was that it would throw the recruit into a full blown panic—firstly because of the shocking sound, and secondly because as a recruit you're unfamiliar with the equipment and it takes forever to figure out how to get the noise to stop! In actuality all that needed to be done to end a "mic bomb" was to move the toggle switch on the sirens to the off position. Under pressure that is extremely difficult especially when your "coach" is laughing uncontrollably at you. In the end everyone inside central headquarters would get irritated, a recruit would get embarrassed, a co-worker would get a good laugh, and most importantly a rite of passage had been fulfilled.

LETTUCE CRISPER LATRINE

Aside from car crashes, my least favorite call to get sent on was the "check the well being of children." Going on those child welfare check calls was like roulette—never knowing what you're going to land on. One of these in particular is burned into my memory for all time.

This incident took place during my field training, so technically to the dispatcher I wasn't really there for protocol reasons. This type of call is a two Officer call, and the other Officer dispatched to this incident also had a recruit, so in reality there were four cops showing up to check on these kids. It turned out there were five kids we were checking on. The oldest turned out to be a fifteen year old boy, and the youngest was about six or seven. This happened during the winter of 2000 and I remember it being pretty cold out. The call itself didn't get dispatched until about 7:00 PM, so it was cold and dark.

When we approached the house it appeared to be abandoned. Upon knocking on the door the fifteen year old boy answered. He was immediately defensive, asking why the hell we were there. The smell coming out of the house was quite literally strong enough to make a person wretch. We explained to him that someone had called 911 for us to come and check out the living conditions. Very reluctantly he let us come inside. The rest of his siblings were all huddled on a couch in the front room under blankets, and the only light in the room was from candles.

We started to ask the routine questions, like where the parents were, and did they have electricity and running water. The eldest explained that he was in charge of the house, and he wasn't sure where his mother was. There was no mention of a father. There was neither electricity, nor running water. All of us knew right then that all of the children were going to have to be placed into emergency foster care. In order to do that everything had to be documented to prove the need for removal from the residence. Well, guess what happened next. The recruits got the task of going room to room with old school Polaroid cameras to document the living conditions. I wish I had the pictures we took that night because words just don't do this story justice.

For starters, there was trash everywhere. I mean everywhere. It was impossible to walk without stepping on trash. This was nothing compared to the horrors we encountered during the rest of the survey. Since there was no running water, there was no flushing the toilet. Therefore, the urine and feces was piled to point of overflowing. Thankfully it was winter; otherwise I cannot imagine how many flies would have been present. The filth was consistent throughout the entire house.

Lastly, we came to the kitchen. One of the things that always had to be documented was whether or not there was food available. Being thorough I opened the refrigerator door which was partially ajar. When I opened the refrigerator door all the way I couldn't comprehend what I was seeing and smelling. Apparently, after the toilet had become full the children had looked for other places to urinate and defecate. As it turned out, one of those places was the lettuce crisper drawer that used to be on the bottom of old refrigerators. I was horrified. I was also angry beyond belief at the mother that put the children in this situation.

Eventually we all made it back to the front room to tell the children we would have to take them somewhere else to stay. What I expected to see was relief from the children. What happened could not be more opposite. The fifteen year old immediately told all of us that "They weren't going anywhere because this was their home." We tried every angle imaginable to reason with him, all to no avail. Finally we told him he was leaving voluntarily or in handcuffs. Without hesitation the young man braced himself in a pose of defiance and didn't move. In my career I cannot recall any tougher of a time trying to put someone into handcuffs. It took four grown men about five full minutes to get one determined fifteen year old into handcuffs. When it was all said and done everyone was exhausted and all the other kids were crying hysterically.

Thankfully we were able to get all five of the kids into the same foster care facility instead of having to separate them. The story ends like this. I and the other recruit were the ones that took the handcuffs off the young man at the foster facility. It is impossible for me to describe the look of defeat in his eyes. Then, my partner recruit did the most amazing thing. He pulled out his wallet and gave the young man a twenty dollar bill as he gave him instructions to buy something for himself and his siblings. The young man began to weep as he took the money. I didn't cry until later when I was alone.

A JEEP FULL OF GUNS

Many of my most memorable incidents happened on Sunday nights. This next one is from early during my five year assignment to the Gang Suppression Unit. Sunday nights tended to be quiet as far as 911 calls go, so they were the perfect night to go looking for trouble. If you go looking for trouble you can usually find it if you try hard enough, and on this Sunday night we were trying unusually hard.

There is something that should be explained about the Omaha Police Gang Unit, at least during the years I worked it. For the most part there were not that many assigned tasks, so the workload was determined by how hard you wanted to work. I loved the job so much that I went to work every day to work as hard as possible. Really, the only hard and fast rule of working the unit was this: Take guns off the streets by targeting gang members. In reality this translates into the business of hunting humans.

On this night my partner and I were hunting one particular gang member of my choosing. He was a member of the Murder Town Gangster Crips, also known by the acronym M.T.G. Don't ask me why, but one quirky thing I always did while on the Gang Unit was to fixate on certain individuals. I suppose the ones I targeted were the most active, or the leaders within their gangs. To me it seemed only logical that if you want to find guns you go after the players. I knew everything about this particular individual: His address, his friends/fellow gang members, and his vehicle.

He drove a late 80's White Jeep Cherokee four door with black accents, so it was relatively easy to spot if you were looking for it. As I already said, we were looking for it. We couldn't find it in the geographic area the Murder Town gang considered their "turf," so we decided to head towards the house where this kid lived, which happened to be on the other side of town in another precinct. This was no big deal since Gang Unit Detectives weren't bound by precinct lines. While en route to his address we saw the Jeep travelling the opposite direction, heading towards where we had just been looking for him.

The street we were travelling on is a divided parkway, so I had to make a u-turn by driving over the center median. Keep in mind we weren't driving a tough Crown Victoria. We were driving an unmarked black Dodge Intrepid equipped with concealed emergency equipment. The engineers at Dodge never intended for the Intrepid to be a patrol car, however it was fast. After negotiating the median we then had to catch up to the jeep. Luckily traffic was light considering it was 9:00 P.M. on a Sunday night. The problem with light traffic however, is that it's really hard not to get spotted when you're the only two cars on the road. We eventually caught up close enough to stay with the Jeep without making it obvious.

We decided to follow the Jeep for a while to see where it was headed, and to maybe get lucky and catch them doing something really stupid. When I say them I mean the four of them. We were able to see that there were four heads in the Jeep so this got me excited. In my experience, any time you put four gangbangers in the same vehicle trouble is definitely afoot. Stopping the Jeep was not going to be a problem since we already had probable cause with a broken left rear tail light. As we tailed them it became obvious they were headed directly for their "turf." It had also become apparent that we had been "made." Our target, the driver of the Jeep was following every traffic law to the letter. Any time you see someone following every traffic law that should tell you they really don't want to get pulled over, because quite frankly it's not easy to follow every traffic statute.

After discussing matters with my partner we made the decision to go ahead and initiate a traffic stop before they got back to their "turf" and comfort zone. I closed the gap between our car and the Jeep and hit the lights. The driver of the jeep didn't even tap the brakes, he just hammered the gas. As it is referred to in police jargon, my partner and I had just taken a big bite from the proverbial "shit sandwich." Here's the problem: At the time our department had a really, really strict policy on police vehicle pursuits. It was even stricter when driving an unmarked police vehicle.

The hardest part of chasing cars is deciding when to get on the radio and let everyone else know you're chasing somebody. The art of chasing a car and never getting on the radio is termed "running silent and deep." This tactic works as long as nothing goes wrong. The problem is that things tend to go wrong during car chases. After about a mile of silent running we finally got on the radio and started the "official" police pursuit. Almost immediately after making our announcement the Jeep turned down a dead end street, which would only mean one thing; this was about to turn from a car chase into a foot chase. That's exactly what happened.

Our primary target, the driver bailed out the door with a chrome pistol in his hand. The other three doors opened at the same time, and now there were four suspects running in four different directions. Now the key to catching four suspects when there are only two cops is this: You have to establish a perimeter and do it quickly. There's another principle that also comes into play. Sometimes it's better to be lucky than good. I will claim that my partner and I were very good, but on this night we were also very lucky.

As it turned out, when the driver of the Jeep and his buddies bailed out on foot they did so about two blocks from an operation being conducted by the Fugitive Unit. So, in addition to every available cop in the precinct coming to our aid because of the pursuit, we now had an extra six or eight cops close by. Furthermore, there was a K-9 unit working that night, so we also had use of a dog.

The first thing my partner and I did after the foot chase started was to establish the perimeter, which happened extremely quickly. We also had to let all the other cops know that at least one of the guys we were looking for had a gun in his hand. As we were trained, assume where there's one gun there's at least one more. The next thing my partner and I did was to physically "clear" the Jeep, just to make sure our head count was accurate and there wasn't a fifth person hiding inside. We had been correct. There had been four people in the jeep. To our surprise, there were more guns in the Jeep then there had been people. There were guns everywhere. The first gun had been in the driver's hand. The second handgun was on the rear passenger floorboard. The third handgun was on the rear driver's side floorboard. The fourth weapon was a 9mm Hi-Point carbine rifle which was on the front passenger floorboard. And just for good measure there was a sawed-off shotgun in the rear cargo area. As it turned out, the driver didn't run far with the gun he was carrying before throwing it down.

Finding the guns was the easy part. Finding all four suspects turned out to be a little more difficult. It was more difficult on the suspects than it was on the cops, since one had to get mauled by the K-9 Officer's German Shepherd before he would surrender. All things considered it couldn't have ended any better. No good guys got hurt, four bad guys went to jail, and we took a whole arsenal of weapons off the streets. If memory serves, I didn't even get in trouble for the car chase. The one thing that bothers me, which I'll never know the answer to, is the question of what they were going to do with all those guns.

RUN TURKEYS, RUN!

This is a tale of one of the dumber stunts I pulled behind the wheel of a cruiser. This incident took place during the fall of my second year on the job. I had just transferred from the northwest precinct to the northeast precinct. The northeast precinct has traditionally been the busiest precinct in Omaha for the more violent crimes. Put another way, the precinct with the most action. This is where I wanted to work, so I was happy even though I had the least amount of seniority in the precinct. When you work the Uniform Patrol Bureau (the street cops) the assignments are handed out by the Patrol Sergeants based upon seniority.

Each of the precincts is subdivided into patrol districts. When a 911 call comes in to the dispatcher it is handled by the Officer assigned to the district from which the call originated. On the night of this story I was assigned to the furthest outlying district in the northeast precinct, district thirty-one. Not many 911 calls ever get dispatched to this district because it's not very heavily populated. It does however have a lot of different places to get lost, goof off, and basically waste time. There are two huge parks in district thirty-one, one of which is on the river and has a large lake.

It was getting late in the shift, and I wanted to get off on time that night, so I wasn't out looking for trouble like usual. Instead I was basically wandering aimlessly through these two city parks wasting time until the end of shift. I had just driven through the park known as Hummel Park. I had been looking for teenagers parked in the dark doing what teenagers do in parked cars. I didn't find any cars so I was on my way to the second park, Dodge Park, which is the one off the river. In this park there are a ton of winding roads that lead to various places. The reason for the bends in the road is due to the shape of the lake. The lake has several little tributaries that branch out from the main body. Well, as I was making my way through the park I came across a large group of wild turkeys standing in the roadway. Feeling mischievous and bored I decided to jack with the poor turkeys. As it turned out, it was poor me.

As the turkeys started to move out of my way I hit the gas and aimed the nose of the cruiser at the center of the group. I wasn't intent on hurting any of them. I was just being a jerk.

Before I realized what had happened I found myself off the pavement and into the grass; and then the lake. Luckily I had just buried the very nose of the cruiser in the lake and it was very shallow, just enough to cover the front push-bars and part of the front tires. Unluckily, I had unbalanced the weight of the cruiser which left little to no traction for the rear drive wheels. My stomach dropped. I could not believe I had been so stupid. More importantly, I had to keep this sort of stupid to myself which meant I had to figure a way out of my predicament.

The first thing I had to do was buy some time. I would have been totally screwed if I would have been dispatched to a 911 call at that point. So, I called the radio dispatcher via the land line and told her to take me out of service for "vehicle maintenance." I figured that wouldn't sound too suspect. Next my brain went into problem solving mode. How in the world was I going to get myself out of this mess? I decided my problem was lack of traction. I needed to find a way to get some traction under my rear wheels. So, I did the only thing I could think to do. I abandoned my cruiser and went into the nearby tree-line to look for fallen branches. Thankfully, cops carry good flashlights.

After numerous trips in and out of the woods I had managed to gather a large pile of various sized tree branches. As I mentioned earlier, this was towards the end of the shift, so pretty soon the next shift would be looking for my cruiser. Time was not on my side. Hastily I began to wedge, stuff, burrow, and shove as many tree branches as I could under the rear wheels. By the time I was done it looked like two miniature beaver dams under the rear of my cruiser. It was time for the moment of truth. Anxiously, I crawled into the cruiser and put it into reverse. Slowly, ever so slowly, I began to feel the rear wheels start to dig in. I kept adding pressure to the gas pedal until WHAM! The rear tires became fully surrounded by tree branches and the cruiser lurched backwards, bouncing over the piles and out of the lake. A wave of relief crept over me. Not only had I managed to get myself un-stuck, I had done it with ten minutes to spare before the call-in for end of shift.

I drove as fast as I could back to the precinct so that I would be ready to hand over the cruiser to the oncoming shift. In my haste I forgot one small detail; the entire front of the cruiser was covered in lake mud! As I transferred the cruiser over to the next cop he looked at me and then the front of the car. He didn't say a word and neither did I.

BODYWORK LESSON

The next two stories deal with me and the same practical joker cop. I didn't find either of the next two stories remotely funny while I was living them. In hindsight, they're pretty amusing to me. The first story about me and this particular cop is pretty short. This goes back to my first crew, when I was just out on my own and scared of every command Officer. Not to mention, I followed every rule out of the Standard Operating Procedure manual to the letter. The other cop in this story did not follow any rules other than his own.

We had been dispatched to some insignificant call together, which turned out to be a whole lot of nothing. Since he was the veteran cop he got to dictate when the call was going to be over. I'll explain what that means. It's tradition after finishing a call to find a parking lot somewhere nearby to "belly-up" the cruisers. It's a stalling tactic to keep from hitting back into service too quickly. If you hit back into service right away, more likely than not you'd be dispatched to another call right away. To prevent that, or at least delay the process meant pulling the cruisers side-by-side in opposition with the driver's windows lined up for purposes of conversation.

I knew we'd be parking somewhere for a while so I followed him to the parking lot of his choosing. I parked first which meant he would spin around in order to line up the cruisers. For whatever reason he didn't get close enough on the first try so he made a second attempt by backing up. True to statistics, most accidents happen In reverse. While backing up he scraped the rear quarter panels of the cruisers causing fairly deep scratches to both cars. I could not believe it. I did have an epiphany though. I now understood why the veteran cops liked to drive old cruisers instead of the newer ones. I was driving a newer cruiser, and he was driving a beater that already had a collection of scratches. To add insult to injury when we finally locked eyes he was laughing. I was livid.

He immediately told me to relax as he pulled the cruisers back apart in order to survey the damage. The next thing he told me was "Don't worry, I got this." I wasn't really sure what the crap he was talking about. I was about to start complaining about having to do paperwork for damaging a cruiser when he started digging through his big patrol bag. A short time later he was headed towards me carrying a black permanent marker and black shoe polish. Without a word he went to work on the scratch on my cruiser, first with the marker then with the shoe polish. By the time he was done I had to admit it didn't look half bad! If you didn't look right at it you'd never see it. After putting his "tools" away he told me simply to just "park it like you would any other night at the end of shift."

I didn't feel too good about it, but I did it. I kept checking the car on the sly for the next couple of nights and slowly the cover-up was starting to fade. By now multiple other cops had driven the cruiser, so there was no way to pin it on me short of telling on myself. That didn't happen. What did happen is that I learned a valuable lesson about items you should always carry in your gear bag.

SUCKER WITH AN EXTRA BADGE

Pay close attention when reading this story because it's kind of hard to follow. Hopefully I can make sense of it on paper. I hadn't been out on my own for more than three maybe four weeks. On the day of this story I had gone to roll-call just like every other day. On this day however, instead of being assigned a cruiser by my Sergeant, I got assigned to the front desk downtown. This was common practice when the front desk was short staffed—low person on seniority got the job for the night. So off to Central Headquarters I went.

I hadn't been down there more than twenty minutes when the phone rang, and of course I had to answer it. To my surprise the person calling was the practical joker cop with the amateur body-work skills. He had a whole practical joke hatched and he needed me to play along to make it work. I should have said no right there. I didn't.

Here's what he wanted me to do. He explained to me that he had found another cop's wallet in the parking lot of the police precinct just before roll call. It happened to be a cop I didn't even know. Most cops carry an additional flat badge in their wallet for various reasons. So far I was lost and didn't see the big deal. Just give the cop his lost wallet. No, that was not the plan. The plan was to have me call the cop's Sergeant with a different story. It would all start with joker cop bringing the wallet down to me at police headquarters. It needs to be noted at this point that directly across from headquarters was a bar frequented by those with alternative lifestyles. My role in the joke was to call the Sergeant and tell him that a Good Samaritan had found the wallet in one of the bathroom stalls of this bar across the street. Again, I should have said no, but I didn't. I agreed.

Thirty minutes later joker cop walked in the front door and handed me the wallet, running through what he wanted me to tell the Sergeant whom I was about to call and lie to. I must have asked him ten times…. "Are you sure this is going to be funny?" He assured me everything was fine, and the precinct Lieutenant was even in on the joke. So I did it. I made the call and told the tale to the Sergeant. The first thing he wanted to know was how many people knew about what had happened. I explained it was just me and the person that found the wallet. The Sergeant praised me repeatedly for "doing the right thing by calling him." He further told me that he would be coming straight down to headquarters to collect the wallet and badge. By this point in the game I was about to have a stroke for agreeing to take part in this prank.

Something that's pretty important to this story is the background of the Sergeant I had just lied to via phone, and then face to face. He was a totally hardcore military man that genuinely had no sense of humor that was detectable. After he left with the wallet and badge I figured that was the end of my involvement. Joke over. Wrong. Joke on me! The very next day MY Sergeant was waiting for me the minute I walked in the door of the precinct building. There were no pleasantries. He simply asked me, "What the hell did you do?" Then he corrected himself and told me he didn't want to know. I was ordered to report directly and immediately to the Sergeant I dealt with the previous day. I thought I was going to puke. I truly believed I was about to lose my career that I had worked so hard to attain.

With my tail between my legs I went to find the Sergeant. What I got when I found him was an ass-chewing like you wouldn't believe; filled with threats. Having been in the military myself I knew how to handle an ass-chewing, so I did. The

Sergeant knew I wasn't the mastermind of the prank, but to my credit I wouldn't give up who was. That got me more yelling and threats. At the end of it all I got off with a verbal warning with the condition that I apologize to the cop who had been the butt of this joke. As I mentioned, I didn't know the guy. There's nothing worse than having to apologize to another cop you don't know—it felt like a violation of the honor code. As I found out later, the ass-chewing I got was nothing compared to the one handed out on the victim of the prank before the precinct Lieutenant had intervened to blow the whistle on the joke. I felt bad, really bad.

IT'S TOO LATE TO GIVE UP NOW

For the Officers on road patrol there are times when you are riding with a partner in a two Officer car, and there are other times when you are riding by yourself. It is obviously way more fun to have a partner in the car with you. Besides having someone to talk to, it also provides the opportunity to take more risks. When I was riding by myself I always made it a point to try and find someone else on the crew willing to ride tandem. This meant even though you were in separate cars you would be driving around essentially following each other. This was almost as good as riding in a two Officer car because your backup Officer was right behind you in the event you got into something good.

Me and a buddy were pulling the tandem tactic one afternoon mid-summer, would have been 2002. It was just after roll-call and we were going to the gas station to get our drinks for the cruisers. We were heading down 30th street which is a major thoroughfare in north Omaha. All of the sudden my buddy who was ahead of me whips a u-turn right in the middle of traffic. I did the same as soon as I was able, and got turned around just in time to see my buddy apparently chasing a newer model Cadillac. I almost got caught up to the two when they made an abrupt right hand turn up a steep side street. When I rounded the turn I saw an abandoned Cadillac rolling backwards down the street, and my buddy running off between some houses. It had all happened in the blink of an eye because I hadn't been that far behind them!

Luckily the Cadillac rolled past the parked cruiser without hitting it and came to rest against an old pine tree. I got stopped and opened my door just in time to hear "I give up!" followed immediately by a blood curdling scream of pure pain. I followed the sounds of the screams between the houses where I found my buddy picking a little guy off of the ground. I say little because he was no more than about five foot two inches tall. Oh, one other thing I noticed about him was that his left arm was bent in half—not at the elbow. By now the little guy was kind of in shock and wasn't howling anymore.

This was one of those chases that went down "silent and deep" so the only witnesses were me, my buddy, and the trees. Of course we had to call a rescue squad to transport the wounded driver to the hospital for his broken wing. We also had to call a tow truck for the Cadillac which turned out to be stolen from a residential burglary. We had to place a call to the Sergeant and give him the most polished, make it sound good story possible. Otherwise, there would have been a lot of paperwork.

When it was all said and done I asked my buddy in the precinct parking lot why he had turned around so abruptly on the Cadillac. He told me that he recognized the driver as a serial burglar whom he had dealt with before. Basically he had played a hunch. In my experience some of the best police work gets done by gut instincts. My buddy then got a huge smile on his face and told me "Wait till you see this!" He started fishing around in the trunk of the cruiser and soon produced the VHS tape from the cruiser camera system. It used to be that the camera systems in the cruisers were nothing more than a VCR mounted in the trunk. Before digital camera systems it was easy to "lose" evidence if a person was so inclined. All it took was removing the old VHS tape and replacing it with a new one. With the modern camera systems it's impossible to hide anything once the camera has seen it.

We went inside the precinct building and rounded up the rest of the crew that was around. My buddy then put the VHS tape from the incident in the VCR that was in the roll-call room. What we watched was both hilarious and disgustingly graphic all at the same time. My buddy was playing the 10-15 seconds that I had missed during the chase when they had turned the corner out of my sight. The camera captured the suspect driver bailing out of the moving Cadillac onto to the pavement. As he launched himself out of the car he braced his fall with his left arm which immediately snapped like a twig. Unbelievably, he rolled a couple times and was back on his feet without missing a step. Then, the rest of the action happens out of the view of the cruiser cam. My buddy had to fill us in on how the chase ended. It turns out the screams of pain I had heard earlier had been caused by my buddy. As my buddy told it, the suspect had given up and turned around, saying "I give up!" My buddy also told me that he had been right behind him at a dead sprint and just decided it was too late to give up now.

   The suspect was five foot two, maybe a hundred-twenty pounds, with a mangled arm. My buddy is six foot two, about two hundred-twenty pounds, and played college rugby. I would have screamed too the way the ending tackle was described to me in painful detail. There are several morals to this story. Firstly, don't get popular with the cops so they recognize you. Secondly, don't break into houses and steal cars. Thirdly, never give up. Cops aren't above a good cheap shot when the street justice requires it.

THAT NICKNAME WILL STICK

I still smile to myself every time I think about this story; for lots of reasons. It was a super hot summer day mid July. Two of us had been dispatched to a "vicious dog call." Nothing worse than having to get out and chase down a dog when the weather is unbearably hot. Nine times out of ten you never found the dog anyway. Dutiful as always, and young and naïve, I parked my car and started checking for the dog on foot. My partner on this call had done the same.

We were traipsing through the back yards and alley behind the call address when this enormous Chow-Chow charged me with murder in its eyes. I had no idea I could draw my duty weapon and fire two shots so quickly. I was terrified, and completely surprised by this dog. My partner had been fifteen feet away from me in the next yard behind a hedge row and hadn't seen any of what just happened. He started yelling as soon as I started shooting. Turns out he was a little surprised as well. I told him "we were 88" I had just shot a dog. But I hadn't shot the dog. I had missed with both shots from near point-blank range. I did however put the dog in a state of shock, as it was now just sitting there doing absolutely nothing. I had accomplished one other thing; I had awoken the dog's owner. The gentleman that owned the dog popped out his back door and called for it. The dog immediately followed the command and ran in the house. The owner never even said a word to me and my partner!

Now as one can assume, the sound of gunfire makes people nervous, so I had to get on the radio and tell the dispatcher the gunfire was from me. This of course prompted our Sergeant to get on the radio to let us know he would be dropping by to see what was happening. Luckily for me, I had the most understanding Sergeant on the entire department. Not long after the Sarge pulled up, I think smoking a cigar. True to nature he was nothing but calm as I recounted the reason for the gunfire. Then he wanted to see the corpse of the vicious dog. I had to explain to him that I had **REALLY** scared the dog into submission and the owner had taken it inside. After he finished laughing, he got on the radio and asked for the Humane Society to be dispatched to our location. So we all waited, Sarge smoking his cigar, me looking sheepish, and my partner glaring at me for scaring the crap out of him for shooting without warning.

After what seemed like forever animal control showed up and knocked on the door to the house with the dog. After making a phone call the Humane Society Officer then returned to the truck with the now docile Chow-Chow on a lead. The stupid mutt jumped in the truck and quietly went down to the pound. It turned out the dog had no license, no vaccinations, and had been complained on before for vicious behavior towards neighborhood kids. This left me, my partner, and our Sergeant standing around three cruisers in the middle of the street. Then Sarge uttered the words that to this day make me smile—"I guess we're done here, hey shooter?" With that, a nickname was given that sticks to this day.

CHOW-CHOW PART TWO

Months had gone by, and I had finally come to grips with the fact that the first discharge of my duty weapon at work had been a complete failure. I knew that mangy Chow-Chow was still alive and laughing at me. Plus, I now had a nickname that I had to painfully explain to others when asked. To my surprise, one afternoon I was checking my mailbox prior to roll-call and found a subpoena for a court case regarding an "unlicensed animal." I went and pulled the reports from the computer and sure enough it was the Chow-Chow debacle.

As it turned out, that mangy mutt had been locked up for several months as the court case kept getting delayed for whatever reasons. Finally, it appeared as though the dog was going to have its day in court. So, on the appointed day and time I showed up in the courtroom to be a witness for the state against the dog's owner. As it turned out I never got called to the stand, but I did stick around because I wanted to see the outcome of this case. The judge was told the details by the City Prosecutor. Then, the Judge had to listen to a litany of excuses by the dog's owner as to why the dog had been unrestrained, not vaccinated, and not licensed on the day I shot at it.

The judge also learned from the Humane Society Officer that the dog had amassed a boarding fee of about $1,500 during the several month stay at the city pound. After learning that fact the Judge had heard enough. It was ordered that thirty days would be given to the dog's owner to get all records and fees taken care of, or the dog was going to be put down. This order was met with much protest by the dog's owner which almost landed him in jail for contempt.

Thirty-one days later I got an e-mail from the Humane Society Officer which simply stated: "The Chow-Chow is dead." Inwardly I smiled to myself. "Shooter" had killed that vicious dog that day in a sense. It just took a lot longer to die than I had planned.

I'M MISSING SOME CUFFS, AND A SUSPECT

I had just gotten partnered with a guy that was newly promoted into the Gang Unit. I was excited because I was told he was a real aggressive younger cop. So, I had a new partner and it was spring time. Perfect, the gangbangers always suffer heavily from cabin fever during the winter months. It's a lot harder to find people to shoot when it's cold out. It was a particularly nice day and people were everywhere. I was trying to get a feel for my new partner, so my intent was to find some action during our shift. I was driving so I decided to take us to Miami Park. This is a city park known to be frequented by 40th Avenue Crips.

True to form as we approached we could see a group of about five guys wearing their blue colors standing by a picnic table in the middle of the park. One of my favorite, make that my all-time favorite activity was chasing guys on foot. I don't know why, I just always loved the foot chases. So, whenever possible I would approach guys on foot so it would be a fair start in the event of a foot chase. When you roll up on guys in the cruiser and they take off running it makes it tons harder because you're starting at a huge disadvantage, having to park and whatnot.

We parked about a half block from the park and walked in on foot. As soon as we got close enough we could see that the group had several open containers of alcohol sitting at their feet. Perfect! No need to establish probable cause for searching these guys since they were now technically under arrest for open containers of alcohol in the public park. Then I got stupid. We were outnumbered two to five against a group of guys known for leading violent lifestyles. In retrospect, the smart move would have been to ask for another cop or two to back us up before taking enforcement action. In our haste I decided to just start cuffing guys. I cuffed the first guy and patted him down, no problem. I cuffed the second guy and patted him down, no problem. I went to grab the third guy, and wouldn't you know it, he pulled a long barreled revolver from out of his hooded sweatshirt and took off running. I was momentarily dazed because I couldn't believe how cool this kid had just played it. After regaining my composure I took off after him. I had caught up to him and was right on his ass about twenty seconds into the chase. I had already put the foot chase out over the radio, and I could hear the sirens of backup Officers screaming our way to help.

As soon as I caught up to the suspect I tried my usual textbook bluff. I yelled at this kid from about ten feet behind him, "you better stop or I'm going to shoot you in the back!" He was still carrying the revolver in his right hand as he was running. Well, my bluff half worked. We were running between two houses at the time and he decided to pitch the revolver in a window well, but he kept running. This just pissed me off because I didn't have time to stop and pick up the gun. As we rounded the corner of a house about twenty seconds later he got tripped up by a small chicken wire fence and went down hard. I was on him immediately. He had the wind knocked out of him and was struggling to breathe. Now I had this kid unarmed and defenseless, so I went to cuff him. One small problem—all my handcuffs were on two guys three blocks away in a park!

I got on the radio to call for my partner to bring me some cuffs. I figured he was still at the park watching the other suspects. As soon as I keyed my microphone and started talking I could hear my radio traffic from somewhere close behind me. I was sitting on top of my suspect who was face down in the mud receiving the occasional kidney punch to keep him docile. I turned around to see my partner standing there with the discarded revolver in one hand, and a pair of his cuffs in the other. I hadn't realized it, but he had followed me the whole way and not made a sound. I was both surprised and relieved to see him. I cuffed the suspect and stood him up so we could walk back to the park. By now other Officers had made it to the park and were watching the other three suspects, one of whom was wearing handcuffs. If you're reading closely then you just caught the problem: There should have been two guys wearing cuffs in that park!

As it turned out, the very first guy I had cuffed decided he wasn't going to stick around for the show. He was gone. Worse yet, the other three guys claimed they didn't know him, and neither did we. To add insult to injury, he had been wearing my favorite pair of very expensive ultra-light titanium cuffs. I never did get those cuffs back or figure out who the guy was. Good for him, he got his little trophy and his own story to tell.

On the way down to Central Headquarters my new partner and I discussed the tactics of what had happened. We both agreed it's a good idea for one person to stay with guys in handcuffs. Apparently, the Officer Safety Committee agreed with our assessment since I ended up getting an official reprimand for letting a prisoner escape. Oh well I say. I lost some handcuffs, big deal. I got an illegal firearm off the streets and out of the hands of a gangbanger. I call that a good days work.

DUDE, YOU ARE SLOW

One of the many things I learned about gangbangers is this: They smoke a lot of weed. Now many of them are still lightning fast for a short distance, but when it comes to long distances forget it. They fade fast. The trick to winning foot chases is therefore pretty simple. Keep them in your sight. As long as you can keep them in sight, odds are you were going to catch them. At least that was always my experience.

This story starts out the same way every day started during my time in the Gang Unit. Get in the cruiser and start looking for the bad guys. Some days it was easy, other days you had to work at it. On this day it was easy. My usual partner had the day off so I was riding with somebody else for the shift. He wasn't really too keen on working hard since it was kind of raining off and on. None-the-less I convinced him to ride around while I drove. We had just started hunting when we found a couple of regulars walking down 16th street by Victor Street. These two streets are ground zero for the Victor Street Bloods. When I say walking, I should add that one of the two was actually limping on his crutches since he had just gotten shot in the leg the week prior.

Crutches or not, you have to use the sidewalk or you're obstructing a public roadway.

At this point let me state one of my favorite axioms of police work: The guys that get shot tend to be the ones that carry guns. Pretty solid logic if you think about it. In any event the axiom was mostly true in this particular instance. The instant we pulled up and got out of the cruiser the guy not on crutches started whining, "We didn't do anything!" I took that as a very strong indicator that they were indeed doing something wrong other than walking in the street. I took about two steps towards the whiner and away he went. I told my partner to stay with Mr. Crutches as I headed off in pursuit. The kid I was chasing was actually pretty fast...for the first fifty yards. At that point he pitched his gun in a yard and kept going.

I now had a dilemma. I could forget the gun and stay on the runner, or I could stop for the gun and most likely lose the runner. I made the split second decision to stop for the gun, which meant I had to take my eyes off the suspect. I had been on the radio putting out the chase details, and remember actually saying "I'm stopping to pick up the gun he threw." Then I continued with the chase. I found over the years you tend to say the strangest things when hopped up on adrenaline. Unfortunately, I had lost sight of my prey. Luckily for me this guy had chosen the wrong way to run. As you run eastbound from 16th Street you hit a huge steep cliff that drops off to a set of railroad tracks. Since I had been putting the details on the radio all the arriving units had done a great job putting up a perimeter for me. It was only a matter of time.

It didn't take long. I found him hiding in the cellar stairs of an abandoned house. What took even less time was for me to start verbally berating this kid. I really let him have it. Actually he wasn't being berated. He was straight out being punked. I explained to him how pathetic it was that a man twice his age had chased him, stopped to pick up the gun he had thrown down, and still caught him! I punked him the entire time it took to drive to Central Headquarters for booking. Did I need to? No. Was it unprofessional? Yes. Did it feel good? Hell yes.

PROPHETIC COFFEE CUP

Before you read this story, I swear to you it's true. Me personally, I don't believe in the supernatural. If you do, then you should enjoy this story. This story involves one of the first shootings I handled when I was still fairly new to the job. I didn't go to the shooting scene; instead I was dispatched to the hospital to make out the original incident report. As the reader you may or may not know that a lot of police work gets done over the phone. By the time I got to the hospital the shooting victim was already in emergency surgery, and many of his family members were in the waiting room.

My first job at the hospital was to ascertain what condition the victim was in, and what the doctor's best guess was at prognosis. I did this in order to relay information to the Homicide Unit to determine whether or not they would be handling the investigation. I was able to learn from the trauma nurses in the emergency room that the victim was not in good shape and it didn't look promising. With that information relayed to the Homicide Unit I started to write out my original incident report. Like I said, a lot of police work gets done over the phone. I first called the dispatcher for some of the details. Then I called one of the cops at the actual shooting scene for more of the facts. Then finally I had to go over to the family and friends and attempt interviews.

    The family and friends were in the surgery waiting room. It was a typical hospital waiting room with couches, tables, T.V.'s, and vending machines. One of the vending machines was for hot beverages like coffee and hot chocolate. I identified the victim's mother and went over to talk to her. As I approached I noted that she was drinking something hot from the vending machine. The cups that were being dispensed by the machine were cardboard with poker hands on them. Playing cards seemed to me to be a funny thing to put on coffee cups, but whatever.

    As I stood there talking to the mother I noticed the exact poker hand on her cup. I know I must have stood there for a moment fixated because I was genuinely shocked. It contained two black Aces, and two black Eights. If you don't play poker, or aren't familiar with this hand then I will explain it to you. This is known in folklore as the "Dead Man's Hand." I thought to myself how inappropriate for a hospital cup. I finished talking to the mother and went to a table in the corner of the room to write. As God is my witness, it wasn't five minutes before the surgeon came out to talk to the family. The victim had died during surgery from his gunshot wounds.

PARKING WOULD HAVE BEEN SMARTER

One of the worst parts of the field training process was working the "A" shift, which is the overnight shift. I don't know how people ever get used to working those hours. It's pure misery to live the vampire lifestyle. Fortunately I only had to work it for five weeks. My coach during those five weeks taught me a lot about how to sleep on duty. I felt bad for the guy. He had five kids and always looked like a zombie. From the first night he was my coach he made me adhere to a strict pattern on how the nightly activities would play out.

When the overnight shift starts there are a few lingering report calls and miscellaneous low priority calls that have to be cleared up by the oncoming shift. Once that's done, it becomes a matter of choice whether or not you want to do anything. Some cops used the time to hunt down drunk drivers. Not my coach. He used the time to catch up on his sleep. And sleep he did, through anything. I swear that's the whole reason he became a Field Training Officer, so that he would have someone to drive him around and listen to the dispatcher. Still, he was a super nice guy so I indulged him. He did have one rule that I had to follow when he was sleeping. I was not allowed to initiate any traffic stops or engage in any sort of risky police work. Translated: Just drive around and listen to the police radio. Actually, he preferred it when I just found a hole and parked.

When you're a recruit cop and you've got this fun cruiser to play with it is really hard to just sit and do nothing. I remember one particular night about four weeks into that field training phase. Everything was on schedule. We had cleared up our 911 calls and it was time for coach's night-night. We went to an old deserted hotel parking lot off of Dodge Street just east of the Westroads mall. This was a favorite hole because it was nicely hidden and centrally located within our precinct. By the time I parked the cruiser my coach was already knocked out. After about an hour of complete and utter silence I decided I'd had enough of nothing.

I crept out of the hole and onto Dodge Street and headed westbound. I had no idea where I was headed; I just had to go somewhere. I remember sticking to the major streets, so as not to accidentally find any kind of crime occurring which would necessitate waking up coach. I must have driven fifty miles just going around in big circles throughout the precinct. I passed several other cops during my travels. Then, all of the sudden I felt the cruiser shake violently and I found myself in the middle of a strip mall parking lot. I hit the brakes hard enough to come to a screeching stop. This proved to be more than even coach could sleep through. He bolted upright from the reclined passenger seat and exclaimed "What just happened?" That was a great question, because I had no idea! I had no idea because I had fallen asleep while driving down the middle of the road and had apparently jumped the curb before coming to rest in the strip mall parking lot.

I have always prided myself on being a quick thinker, and in this case I shined. The strip mall we landed in was on the western outskirts of the city, so there were wooded areas nearby. I proceeded to tell my coach how I had been driving down 144th Street when all of the sudden a deer had ran into the roadway right in front of me! I explained how I had taken evasive action to avoid hitting the animal which had necessitated me jumping the curb to the strip mall parking lot. Not only did I NOT get in trouble, I got high marks for driving on my daily evaluation.

AGAINST ALL ODDS GUN CATCH

I have to preface this next story with an admonishment. This story is in no way any sort of commentary, nor meant to slander or offend any particular group, individual, or lifestyle choice. This story is just one of my stories—nothing more.

By about my third year on the Gang Unit I had gotten pretty cocky about my ability to find illegal guns on the street. Finding guns was what I lived for. I literally could not get enough of the adrenaline rush that came with the foot chases, car chases, and fights when you knew you were going to find a gun at the end. To be honest, there are so many illegal firearms on the streets of Omaha it is not hard to find them if you try.

It was a slow summer night and we were having trouble finding any gangbangers out and about. So, we took to giving each other crap in the cruiser to pass the time. We also had a third cop in the cruiser that night. I don't remember if somebody on the crew was sick, or we were short a cruiser, but whatever the reason there was three of us riding around. At some point in the conversation a challenge got thrown down towards me. I was driving, so it was my responsibility to find the action for the night. On this night the action was going to be tough. I had been running my mouth that I could find a gun any time I wanted. Well, my partners decided to shut me up by creating the impossible gun challenge. They had concocted a scenario for which they were certain I couldn't succeed.

These were the terms of the challenge: I had to arrest a female on a gun charge...and she had to be a lesbian. Not one to ever back down from a challenge I of course accepted. To myself I was thinking, "How in the world am I going to pull this one off!" So, with the gauntlet thrown down I went about the task of finding a lesbian with a gun. I decided to go to the most recently active part of town for gun violence—the turf of the 40th Avenue Crips. We were actually on 41st Street heading southbound when we came across of all things, a handicapped parking violation. A little old lady lived on the street and she had somehow gotten her own handicapped spot. Well, some twenty-something was parked in the stall without a handicap placard so I decided to stop. What the heck, probable cause is probable cause.

I approached on the passenger side of the car where she was standing with the door open. As soon as I got close enough to converse I could smell the weed coming from the car. When I looked in I could see a blunt still burning in the ashtray. I asked the lady if it was her car and she indicated that it was. I told her I really didn't care about the weed, but that I would have to give her a ticket. She pleaded with me not to give her the ticket because she was visiting from out of town and would be leaving prior to any future court date. I told her I would think about it as long as I didn't find anything else in the car. At that point she began to act really nervous. This could get interesting I thought to myself. During this whole process my two partners were just standing there observing the events unfolding.

With that I began to search the car. Finding nothing under the seats I started opening the compartments. First the center console armrest, and then the glove compartment. When I opened the glove compartment what did I see? That's right! I had found a small black semi-automatic handgun. I began to feel a glimmer of hope. I was halfway to beating the challenge. Since there was now a gun involved I cuffed the lady and had her sit down on the curb next to the car. I verbally mirandized her and began my line of questioning. She gave up the words I wanted to hear. The gun wasn't hers, "It belonged to her girlfriend." As soon as she said it I looked over at my partners who were both standing there dumbfounded. Me, I had to have been looking smug at that point.

Feeling almost guilty I decided to cut the lady as much of a break as I could. I wrote her a ticket for a city ordinance prohibiting carrying loaded firearms in vehicles. I did have to impound the gun as evidence. I also gave the lady instructions on how to contact the city prosecutor so she could resolve the issue before she had to leave town.

With our business done, my partners and I got back in our cruiser and drove off. We didn't make it to the end of the block before we were all laughing hysterically. I proclaimed myself to be a legend, even if it was only my opinion.

DIDN'T SEE THAT COMING

One thing that never ceased to amaze me was how many crimes happened literally a stone's throw from the northeast precinct building. The precinct sits on the corner of 30th and Taylor Streets. One block to the north is Ames Avenue, the major east—west street for the precinct. On the corner of 30th and Ames there is a gas station, a McDonald's, a grocery store, and another gas station. For unknown reasons this corner was the social epicenter for the precinct every Friday and Saturday nights.

Things would get so out of control the gas station owner for the longest time paid two off duty cops in uniform to stand in the parking lot on the weekends from eleven P.M. until 3 A.M. at the rate of $30/hour. Most of the time I was one of the off-duty cops that worked the shift. When I say crimes, I mean CRIMES. This corner had homicides, shootings, gang brawls, near riots, and at least one Officer-involved shooting that I can remember. All this took place less than one block from the precinct—damn near anarchy. This is just the activity in the parking lots. Up and down 30th Street and Ames Avenue there were processions of carloads of restless people looking to get into trouble.

At the end of the shift one Friday night my partner and I were coming back to the precinct to unload the cruiser when I got the bright idea to just drive through the gas station parking lot for really no reason other than to annoy the crowd that was gathered. I distinctly remember my partner protesting my action. As we were navigating the crowd I saw three guys standing next to a car smoking weed like nobody's business. Now I was known for turning a blind eye to a lot of petty crimes, but to smoke so blatantly in public demanded we stop.

Quite honestly, since it was the end of shift I was going to just take their weed away and pitch it. So that is what I set out to do. It was a cool night so all three guys had on hooded sweatshirts. This is where I interject once again that God looks out for cops. What we should have done was cuff the three guys, search them, and then seize any weed. We started with the closest guy and searched him to make sure he didn't have any baggies of weed in his pockets. Second guy, the same drill. The third guy had patiently waited his turn with his hands in the front of his hooded sweatshirt. This really should have been the world's biggest clue. I don't know if my partner and I missed it because we were tired, complacent, bored, it really didn't matter. The instant I reached for the third guy he pulled a mid-sized Glock out of his hooded sweatshirt and took off. He had been standing there the whole time with his hand on the gun. Had he wanted to he could have shot both me and my partner before we would have known what hit us! In any event, now the chase was on.

Remember, it was the end of the shift, so every cop was driving right by us on the way to the precinct. Thankfully the suspect pitched the gun fairly early in the chase and a cop was right there to witness it and pick up the gun. Believe me; if a cop hadn't been right there, that gun would have been in the hands of its next owner given the number of people standing around watching. The suspect ended up being caught about two blocks away. As it turned out, he was a bit of a habitual criminal and he got Federally Indicted. He got ten years for that gun charge. Me, I learned to make everyone take their hands out of their pockets immediately when I wanted to talk.

GO AHEAD AND TAKE A PISS

One of the smartest things you can do as a rookie cop is to watch and learn from the veteran Officers. I was very fortunate early in my career to ride with a very salty veteran. I rode with him every day for six months. I learned more tricks during those six months than I did at any other point during my career. This story is one of my personal favorites.

It was summertime and it was dark out. We had been patrolling an area around 18th and Sahler Streets, an area controlled by the Sahler Block Crips. As we rolled through the area we came across a group of about a dozen guys all crowded around one car. I think I've said it before, but if not then I'm saying it now: If there are that many guys standing in a group then someone or multiple people have guns. We stopped about twenty-five yards away and walked up on foot. There's no sense being trapped in your cruiser if you're going to be shot at. As soon as we reached the group one of the bangers started whining that he really had to take a piss! I had just told the guy to hold it when my partner interrupted and said "If he's gotta piss, then let him go piss over by that tree." As he said it he pointed to a big old pine tree across the street. As the guy started to walk away my partner told him calmly, "Be sure you come back when you're done."

While the guy was pissing we shook down the rest of the group and didn't find anybody holding any contraband. After a couple of minutes the guy pissing returned as he had been told. As soon as the guy was within reach my partner grabbed him and cuffed him in one smooth motion. As the guy was crying foul my partner handed the guy over to me and told me to hold on tight to him. I was a bit confused but did as I was told. The guy was pretty tiny so holding onto him wasn't a challenge. My partner then walked over across the street to the tree where the guy had supposedly just pissed. I saw my partner shining his flashlight around on the ground, and then the beam locked on something I couldn't see from where I was standing.

My partner walked back over to where we were all standing and told the rest of the bangers to take off down the street. Then he motioned for me to follow him. I followed him with the suspect in tow. As we reached the "piss tree" my partner shined his flashlight over a chain link fence that was next to the tree. There, illuminated by my partner's flashlight was a small black semi-auto handgun and the biggest ball of crack-cocaine I had personally ever seen. The suspect immediately started screaming, "But you let me piss!" Over and over he kept wailing like a broken record, "You let me piss!" Now I'm not sure if he thought that was his criminal defense, but I assure you it was not a viable one. My partner even told him as much.

My partner put on some rubber gloves and retrieved the gun and the crack while I searched the suspect. It turned out the only thing he hadn't thrown by the tree was the almost $2,000.00 in cash he had crammed in his pants pockets. The drive to Central Headquarters for booking was miserable. The entire drive was nothing but "You let me piss!" That guy got Federally Indicted on weapons and narcotics charges.

THAT'S WHY THEY'RE NUMBERED

Here's another story from my travels with the salty vet. This story also involves trickery. I swear it's a good thing he is a cop, because he would be a tremendous criminal if he chose to be. Anyway, we were doing nothing, just driving. Some of the best police work happens when you're doing nothing; just keeping your eyes open. We both saw the kid at the same time. It was dusk out and we were coming at him from the opposite direction. He was walking down the sidewalk carrying a bank deposit bag like the ones businesses use for their nightly deposit. We drove by and pretended not to notice, but as soon as we passed him we were glued to the rear view mirror. The kid's conscience had gotten to him and he took off running.

It didn't take us long for us to catch him and recover the bank bag. He was young, about sixteen years old. We put him in the cruiser and took him to the precinct to figure out the story. At the precinct there are interview rooms. We put him in one and let him sit while we examined the contents of the bank bag. The deposit slip with the business name was conspicuously missing.

The only thing in the bag was cash. This kid we had in custody didn't seem overly bright, nor did he seem like he had many street smarts. I think that's what gave my partner his plan. As usual he kept me in the dark, which I think gave him some strange satisfaction. No, he just really enjoyed being a mentor and making me learn from him.

He told me to watch the kid while he ran across the parking lot to the ATM at the bank. Totally confused, I again just did as I was told. He was back in a couple of minutes with a huge grin on his face. He asked me if we were ready to interview the kid, to which I said yes since I still didn't know what he was planning. We went into the interview room and my partner silently started laying out twenty-dollar bills on the table in front of the kid. Then he just sat there. We all just sat there. Finally he asked the kid, "Do you notice anything about the bills in front of you?" The kid replied "No." Honestly, it took a while for me to figure it out. The bills my partner had laid on the table weren't the ones from the bank bag. They were the ones he had just taken out of the ATM from his own bank account. What my partner wanted us to notice was the fact that the bills were in sequential order by the serial number. How brilliant was that? My partner then bluffed the kid into believing the bills were recorded by the business that deposited them, or some such nonsense. Whatever the case, the kid caved.

He went on to tell us the story how he had been walking by the bank as somebody was making their deposit. He told us the bag didn't go into the depository like it was supposed to and that the bag had fallen onto the ground after the car drove off. He admitted to picking up the bag and walking off with it. He even went so far as to take us to the spot where he had pitched the deposit slip with the business information on it. By the time it was all said and done we were able to reach the person from the business and get their money back to them. The kid got a break for his honesty and got a ticket instead of going to the juvenile detention facility. When I asked my partner how he knew the ATM bills would be sequential he just smiled and said "I guessed."

DON'T BRING A SHOVEL TO A TASER FIGHT

This story is two things: short and funny. Well, it was funny when it happened. I don't know if it's going to be funny in print. The subject matter is the all too common and annoying 911 dispatch to deal with an unruly drunk. In this case the drunk was a frequent flyer, meaning somebody was always calling him in for being a general pain in the ass. We dealt with this guy so often we all knew him by name. On this particular night he was over at a "friend's house" refusing to leave. When we got to the house we could hear him inside making a fuss. The owner of the house came out to meet us and tell us what we already knew. The story was always the same. Our guy was fine until he had too much to drink and started picking fights with everybody. So, as usual it was our job to get him out of the house.

As it turned out he was acting unusually badly this night. He knew we were outside waiting for him. He also knew that the minute he came out he was going to detox, which meant his party was over for the night. He had decided he wasn't done partying so we were actually going to have to physically deal with him. From experience I'd learned that if you had to fight, don't do it inside. Always take the fight outside whenever possible. My partner on this call was on the same page. My partner had also just received his taser certification and was itching to taze the first candidate.

After a long stretch of begging, pleading, threatening, and ordering our drunken buddy to come outside we finally got our wish. He stumbled out the front door cussing us with a string of foul language you wouldn't want your mother to hear. This was no surprise; in fact it was part of the routine. I was waiting for him at the bottom of the porch steps, while my partner waited on the side of the porch at a perpendicular angle. What our drunk did next was unexpected.

From somewhere on the porch he managed to produce a spade shovel, which he promptly raised over his head like he was going to hit me. Before I could step back I heard the sound of a "pop" and then the sound of electricity as it coursed into our drunk. My partner tased our guy the minute he raised the shovel over his head. I don't know if you've ever seen a taser in action; it's comical to watch. Two barbed darts with wire leads shoot from the taser by an explosive charge. If the darts both find their mark then the results are instantaneous. In this case my partner's aim was true. Our drunk's body went immediately rigid and he was frozen like a statue with a shovel raised over his head. The only thing the taser couldn't change was physics. Specifically, a body in motion tends to stay in motion. When the taser hit our guy he had been stumbling towards me and was right at the edge of the steps. His forward momentum carried him down the four or five porch steps and he landed face first next to me on the sidewalk, still frozen like a statue. After five seconds the taser cycled off and our guy had the power of speech once again. He didn't really say anything though, he more or less just groaned from his resting place on the pavement.

The taser ended the party. Our drunk was now completely co-operative and willing to do whatever was asked of him. Unfortunately during his fall he had gotten a little scuffed up. Detox won't accept somebody that's scuffed up unless you take them to the hospital first to get medically cleared. There was no way we were going to do that. The contact ended like this: "We're going to let you go, but if we have to come back we're going to shoot you with the taser again." Problem solved at least for that night.

THE SHOES DIDN'T MOVE

Sometimes on the job I saw things that I didn't immediately believe, like my eyes were playing tricks on me. This is one of those instances. It was a homicide scene, only I didn't realize that when I was staring right at it. It happened in the parking lot just north of the precinct building. It came out with alert tones by dispatch as a "shooting." Any priority one 911 calls like a shooting, cutting, kidnapping, sexual assault in progress, etc. get alert tones prior to the information being relayed by the dispatcher. I was riding by myself and had just pulled out of the precinct parking lot. When the dispatcher put out the address of the shooting I got confused...I was at the exact address the dispatcher was citing. I didn't see anything going on. This can't be right I thought to myself. I pulled into the parking lot next to the McDonald's and unwittingly drove right on top of the shooting scene.

I stopped the cruiser and got out to inspect the only things I could see in the parking lot; a pair of blue and yellow Nike basketball shoes. I got on the radio and told the dispatcher I was on the call location but couldn't find the victim. Radio then advised the victim had just shown up at the hospital. I walked over and took a good look at the shoes. They were unlaced and lined up just like they would be if somebody was wearing them. Then I saw the blood. It was just a few drops on the concrete surrounding the shoes. I was still a little perplexed, but at least I was confident I had the right location. I moved my cruiser and began stringing up crime scene tape to isolate the scene. Then it dawned on me. This is a parking lot that should have been packed with people at this time of night and it was a ghost-town! This is not an uncommon occurrence when someone gets shot; not one witness to be found.

After stringing the crime scene tape I got a message from the dispatcher to "call radio." When I called the dispatcher she informed me that the victim died on the way to the hospital and I was supposed to secure the scene until the Homicide Detectives got there. When the Detectives got there I showed them what I had for a scene. Finally I got my explanation regarding the shoes. After being shot, the victim's buddies had thrown him into a car and driven him to the hospital themselves. As they reported it to Detectives at the hospital, the gunshots had literally blown the victim out of his shoes. The shoes were in the exact position where the victim had been when he was shot. They explained they left the shoes there because they were in a hurry and knew their buddy was in bad shape. Live and learn, live and learn.

NEW YEAR'S AT HANK'S PLACE

For about the first five years of my career I couldn't get enough of police work. When I wasn't working on-duty I was working off-duty. I mean why not? Most places paid $25—30 dollars an hour so it was easy money in my pocket. One of the places I worked off-duty was a bar called Hank's Place. It was a dive located at 40th and Ames Avenue. Chances were good most nights that at least one fight would break out at closing. This was also the kind of bar that the bouncers pat you down for weapons before letting you in. I didn't care. As long as they paid I'd show up and stand at the front door with the bouncers. I wasn't the only cop. It was actually my good friend who had organized this job with the bar owner, so the two of us always worked together.

It was New Year's Eve 2006, so where else would I be? Not out celebrating, I was at work at Hank's Place with my buddy. It was unusually cold that night, so instead of standing at the front door we had decided to sit in my partner's truck in the parking lot. So there we sat with the truck running, heat on full blast, with the windows cracked waiting for the sound of trouble from the bar. Our parking spot was around the corner on the side of the bar, so we couldn't actually see the front door. It was about 11:30 so the two of us were waiting for the phenomenon that occurs only in north Omaha on New Year's Eve—the celebratory gunfire.

For about forty-five minutes up to and just after midnight on New Year's north Omaha sounds like a warzone. I spent the year of 2003 in Iraq, so believe me I know what I'm talking about. It's really quite the tradition. Everyone who is so inclined steps out onto their yard and fires their weapons into the air. It's so bad that many Patrol Sergeants make their crews stay in the parking lot until the shootings over. After all, those bullets have to come down somewhere.

So there we sat in his truck listening to the gunfire which was literally going on all around us throughout the precinct. We made a game of guessing what caliber of guns we were hearing. It was easy to distinguish the handguns and shotguns from the rifles, especially the SKS's and AK-47's. As we sat there the time approached midnight. At the stroke of midnight the gunfire always intensified until it sounded like the Fourth of July for about five minutes. Right at midnight my buddy and I were just about to shake hands and wish each other Happy New Year's when all of the sudden nine shots go off seemingly right next to the truck! In all seriousness my buddy and I were both trying to squeeze under the dashboard of the truck. Then we decided we better get out of the truck so we wouldn't be sitting targets! We bailed out of the truck and ran to the side of the building and put our backs against the wall. Then we waited. Finally at about ten minutes after midnight the shooting had diminished to just occasional shots.

We were both kind of pissed now that the shock and fear had subsided. We decided to look around for any signs that would indicate the location of the gunfire that scared the piss out of us. It took all of about thirty seconds to find the spot. Right there on the ground in front of the door to the bar laid nine .380 caliber shell casings. Apparently someone inside the bar had been armed. For all we knew it was one of the bouncers. That was the last year I worked New Year's at Hank's.

ANOTHER NEW YEAR'S

On the New Year's Eve theme; here's the saga of 2007. I was on the Gang Unit and we were working all night. As I explained before, midnight in north Omaha brings with it the tradition of celebratory gunfire. Two of the other Detectives on the unit had parked to watch a particular problem house. They had parked far enough away to observe, but not so close as to be obvious. Right on schedule, three of the occupants of the house exited at midnight and started shooting into the air from the porch. As a unit we had been looking for a good reason to get into this house because we all knew it was a gang house, and we assumed we'd find some good criminal activity happening inside. Thanks to the idiocy of the residents we had just gotten our reason to kick the door in.

The two Detectives that witnessed the gunfire got the hard job. They had to write the search warrant and find a judge to sign it. The rest of us on the unit got the easy, albeit boring job of securing the house until it was time to execute the warrant. Thankfully it wasn't too cold that year because we ended up standing outside for several hours. The problem with securing a house for that long is that the people inside know you're coming so they have nothing but time to hide what they don't want found.

Regarding search warrants: the house being searched will get messed up. Every drawer gets emptied, every bed gets flipped, carpets get pulled up, cereal boxes get dumped, and you can imagine the rest. For all intents and purposes the inside looks like a tornado struck when it's all said and done. This is especially true when the drugs and guns are hidden really well. We didn't know if drugs were in the house, but the search warrant clearly stated there were three guns to be found and seized. This meant we couldn't leave until we had at least three guns in our possession.

Sometimes you can convince the occupants of a house to voluntarily give up the goods and spare the tornado search. This case did not turn out to be one of those cases. It really doesn't make much sense if you think about—when you're caught, you're caught. Why not make the process as painless as possible? In any event, we had to do it the hard way. When I say hard way I mean we had to get dirty to find what we were looking for. During the time it took to get the search warrant signed the occupants of the house had buried all the illegal items in the insulation in the attic crawlspace. Digging through insulation sucks. In the end it was worth it. Instead of three guns we ended up finding five guns, and two pounds of weed. That's how you celebrate New Year's.

GONNA NEED A SCALP SURGEON

Back in 2001 Omaha had a serial robber that became public enemy number one. The guy had a raging methamphetamine addiction and decided that robbery was the easiest way to get cash. I don't have the exact number of robberies and car thefts he committed during his reign of terror, but I can say with all certainty the numbers were well into the double digits. The number thirty comes to mind if I had to make my best guess. The time span for the entire spree really wasn't that long since he was committing a robbery daily, sometimes twice daily.

The Detectives had him identified early into the crime spree, but he was slick and fast. By the time the victims could call 911 he was in a car and on the way out of the area. I'll describe his M.O. because it was pretty interesting. For starters he was always in a different car, which made him hard to track. Secondly, he always picked businesses where he was certain no one would try and be a hero. I personally got pretty close to catching him on one instance when he robbed a day old bread store staffed by two elderly ladies. Lastly, instead of using a gun or a knife like most robbers, he used a syringe which he claimed was tainted with H.I.V.

I think I mentioned before how strict the Omaha Police pursuit policy used to be. Well, for this guy the rules were relaxed a bit, giving any cop with a reasonable chance to catch him the ability to chase. Eventually, that is what happened. One of the Traffic Unit cops spotted the bad guy near 90th and Dodge Street around 3:00 in the afternoon in the middle of the week. Back then, the precinct for the northwest quadrant of the city wasn't far from 90th and Dodge. I had just left the building so I was able to get really close to the chase before it ended in one of the nearby residential neighborhoods. Like most car chases it transitioned at the end to a foot chase.

Being cranked up on meth apparently gave the bad guy at least a little advantage because he was able to temporarily lose his pursuers in the foot chase. It was irrelevant because every cop in the city wanted a piece of this guy and a perimeter was established really quickly around the foot chase. Once you have a good perimeter the advantage shifts to the cops. Knowing you have the suspect pinned down inside a perimeter allows the command time to gather the appropriate resources. For this type of a situation, the ideal resource is a **K-9 Unit**.

The tracking went smoothly and the dog, a particularly aggressive service dog, pinned the suspect down in a hedgerow along some citizen's front porch. The suspect made one last ditch effort to bargain his way out of his capture. He placed his syringe to his neck and threatened to blow an air bubble into an artery. I had made it right up to the scene by that point, but I couldn't see the suspect because there were so many cops standing around! It was at that point that the K-9 handler loosed his hound. Now the service animals will bite the first available target on the suspect. In this case it was the suspect's head. It can only be described as a mauling. The dog extricated the suspect completely from the hedgerow by pulling him out by the head. By the time we could see the suspect it looked like his scalp was some type of cheap hairpiece lying on top of his head.

Of course the taxpayers had to pay for the surgery to re-attach the suspect's scalp. I wish I had a copy of the mugshot from that arrest because that picture is legendary. To describe it is impossible. The closest description I can give is to picture someone's head wrapped entirely in blood stained gauze wrap with the most pitiful look imaginable on the person's face. Tax dollars well spent if you ask me.

RETIRE THAT CRUISER

Typically in every precinct there is a cruiser designated for each patrol district. These are the most roadworthy and generally the newest. But, the way cops drive, these cars also get broken a lot. Because of that fact each precinct has a reserve fleet of clunkers for back-ups when one of the new cars is in the shop. Having to drive one of the back-up cars was never fun. Usually the worst part was the smell—not fresh. These cars usually had well over 100,000 miles on them as well which meant you felt every bump on the road.

Working the northeast precinct one afternoon with my partner we found that our normal cruiser was in the shop, leaving us to pick from the row of clunkers. We did, and then headed out to start our shift. It was not fifteen minutes into the shift when we saw a Cadillac moving erratically through traffic on Ames Avenue. We turned around on it as soon as it passed us and got behind it. The driver immediately took note of us and started to speed up. We caught up to the car, barely, and turned on the lights. It was plainly clear from the git-go that this guy wasn't going to stop. We had no choice we had to declare it a pursuit since it was broad daylight with too many witnesses. One other thing was plainly clear; our piece of crap cruiser couldn't hang with the fleeing Cadillac! As we stayed in the chase the gap widened and it was clear the driver was circling a particular area, all the while talking on his cell phone.

The chase continued to our embarrassment, because one by one our co-workers started to **PASS** us as we all chased the Cadillac. There is nothing more humiliating then to be passed during your own car chase! Eventually the driver bailed out and ran into a house. He didn't stay in the house for more than a few seconds before exiting the front door and surrendering. He of course wouldn't explain why he had run into the house. He further would not disclose his relationship to the young lady at the house. She was co-operative and signed a permission to search form, knowing full well we weren't going to find anything, which we didn't.

I'll explain what happened. The driver of the Cadillac was a seasoned veteran criminal. He had circled the same area during the pursuit waiting for his girlfriend to pick up the phone. As soon as she did he knew he was safe to stop and run inside. He was inside just long enough to flush the drugs he had been carrying. He knew full well he was going to get a laundry list of charges due to the pursuit, but none of those would compare to getting caught with the crack, or pills, or whatever it was he flushed. That is as they say "a cost of doing business." For the record, I don't think that piece of crap cruiser ever got driven again.

DOORS DON'T WORK LIKE THAT

I was with my usual partner at the time, working northeast precinct. It was a beautiful day out and we had made the joint decision to work hard that day. Some days we worked harder than others. We were doing our thing, riding around looking for the big fish. Before long we spotted a rust colored Jeep with five or six younger looking guys in it. We decided it looked promising so we took off after them. They apparently didn't want to talk to us because they took off away from us before we even turned on the lights. Now they had our full interest, so we decided to use the "silent and deep" approach to chasing them. If you remember that's chasing a car without using your lights and sirens. Running silent is risky, but sometimes very rewarding as long as nothing goes wrong.

The Jeep was still way ahead of us when all of the sudden it pulled down a gravel access road behind a car wash. They were picking up speed and then BOOM! They hit a wooden utility pole head on causing the transformer at the top to blow. The Jeep literally bounced backwards from the pole after the collision. This would be an instance of something going wrong. By the time we caught up to the Jeep we found five very dazed teenagers inside trying to figure out if they were hurt or not. Luckily for my partner and me nobody was claiming any injuries and we didn't see any blood. Unfortunately we were going to have to call our Sergeant on this one due to the power outage we had caused.

As it turned out the teen driving the Jeep was trying to evade us because he didn't have a driver's license. We gave him a ticket, which was nothing compared to what he was going to get at home for wrecking the jeep which was now un-drivable. So we kicked all the kids loose from the scene and waited for the tow truck to haul away the wreckage. We still hadn't called our Sergeant yet when the tow truck arrived. Furthermore, our cruiser was blocking the tow driver's access. My partner got in the cruiser and was trying to call Sarge and drive at the same time. In his distraction he started backing the cruiser with his driver's door wide open. As he backed up the open door caught a side hill and bent backwards the wrong direction on the door hinges. He didn't stop cussing for a solid five minutes. We tried to close the door, but it wasn't even close. The door had bent the front fender which was now holding the door open. All that can be said for that day was we accomplished what we set out to do—work hard. Too bad all the hard work entailed endless police reports documenting our stupidity.

CRACK SPIT-WAD

This story and the next one are on the topic of putting crack-cocaine in your mouth. Don't do that by the way. The story deals with a traffic stop gone bad. My partner and I had stopped a car for some minor violation. We didn't care about the traffic infraction. We were more interested in the fact we had seen the same vehicle several times throughout the night in an area known for open narcotics dealings. Our guess was the occupants were dealing crack-cocaine from the car.

The car pulled over for us, very slowly. Pulling over slowly can be an indicator that something is being hidden inside the car. As soon as the vehicle stopped my partner and I both made our way up to the car as fast as we could while still being tactical. All I had time to process was that the driver was a female, and the passenger was a male. Then, my partner started yelling—"He's eating it, he's eating it!" I reacted immediately by opening the passenger door; yanking the passenger out onto his feet. Thankfully he hadn't been wearing a seat belt. As soon as he was upright I could see he indeed appeared to be chewing on something. I assumed it was crack and I didn't want him to get it swallowed. I got behind him and put him in a Lateral Vascular Neck Restraint—L.V.N.R. This is nothing more than fancy police jargon for a chokehold. The guy wasn't very tall so I put my back against the car and used leverage to my advantage. He was either going to spit the crack out or I was going to render him unconscious and pull it from his mouth myself.

The guy was squirming for all he was worth so I couldn't get the proper placement around his neck. By that point I was holding him off the ground by his head. All of the sudden my partner materialized in front of me, taser drawn. He was nice enough to give us the verbal warning that he was going to deploy the taser. In theory the taser is only supposed to shock the person hit by the taser probes. In any event I braced myself expecting to get shocked as well. Then it happened; my partner pulled the trigger and out came the probes with their 50,000 volts of electricity. My partner was at near point blank range so both probes hit the suspect directly in the chest. The suspect went rigid and I didn't feel a thing! As soon as the taser cycled through its five second shock I felt the suspect go partially limp in my grasp. I released tension on my chokehold, and as soon as I did the suspect launched the crack from his mouth like a giant spit-wad.

    I put him in handcuffs and secured him in the cruiser. Luckily for us it was still daylight since the crack-wad had been spit into a grassy field next to the suspect's car. A couple more cops had shown up as the suspect was being tazed, so they stuck around to help us look for our evidence. By the time we found it none of us could believe how far he had spit that bag of crack. We didn't walk it off or measure, but it must have been twenty feet. I was just glad the taser manufacturer was correct about me not feeling the shock.

FIREMAN TEN-COUNT

This is another story about why you shouldn't put crack in your mouth. I was on the Gang Unit and riding around with my long time partner. We were out hunting, just like every other night. It doesn't matter how many gangbangers you arrest there's always more the next day. We were patrolling an area controlled by the Flatland Bloods, down in east Omaha around 16th and Emmet Streets. My partner alerted me to a Chevy Tahoe he had information about parked in an apartment complex we had just passed. My partner liked to work the confidential informants, so he was always getting bits of intel from his snitches. My partner told me he thought the Tahoe was occupied. Not having any real probable cause to make contact we decided to pull into the parking lot anyway, just to "sweat" the occupant.

As soon as we pulled in behind the Tahoe we could see the driver furiously shoving something quite large in his mouth. He then exited the vehicle and tried to run into one of the apartment units. Now we had a reason to make contact with our target. My partner snagged him and put him in the Lateral Vascular Neck Constraint. He couldn't get a good hold on the guy so I started helping with knee strikes to the side of his leg, figuring that would soften the suspect's resolve. It didn't. This guy would not give up the contents of his mouth. I could tell whatever was in his mouth was big. If it was crack in his mouth it was probably enough to kill him if he managed to swallow it. If he couldn't swallow it, then he would probably choke on it!

My partner had a good enough hold on the guy I wasn't worried about him getting away. So, I took a quick break from the action and requested a rescue squad over the radio. Then it became a waiting game. The suspect and my partner were both getting tired and they had actually gone to the ground. Eventually the guys from the fire department showed up and I briefed them on what was happening. We were a good twelve minutes into the fight by that point, so something needed to happen.

Finally the Captain on the squad asked me if I thought it would be a medical emergency if the guy was able to swallow the contents of his mouth. I told him yes, it appeared to be a pretty big baggie of crack. The Captain took charge. He told my partner to roll the suspect onto his stomach and then get the hell out of the way. The instant my partner was clear the Captain delivered an atomic knee drop square in the middle of the suspect's back. The Captain was a big guy, so I know it hurt. It also knocked every bit of air out of the suspect's body, and I think he temporarily lost consciousness. Finally, the baggie came out. The instant I saw it I grabbed the suspect and pulled him across the sidewalk and out of reach of the baggie. He was totally exhausted so putting the cuffs on was no problem.

We had been right all along; there had been enough crack in his mouth to kill him. I forget the exact weight but it was somewhere between a quarter and a half an ounce.

SCARED TO THE GROUND BY THE SOUND

Working the Gang Unit didn't come with a lot of responsibilities, but occasionally events would come up that demanded the unit's attention. For example, gang funerals and anniversaries were two events that always got attention. Any time a gangbanger would get killed there would traditionally be a memorial erected on the site where death occurred. Then, furthering tradition, people would gather at the memorial on the anniversary of the death.

The unit was working one such anniversary of a former member of the Camden Block Crips. The location was the end of Camden Street at about 29th Street where it comes to a dead end. It was the middle of the summer so we assumed it would be a big turnout, which it was. The problem with putting too many members of the same gang in one place is that it draws attention from rival gangs. So by default we would get stuck basically babysitting the event to make sure that no gunplay occurred. The anniversary party we were working was turning into an all day event. We had started supervising around noon, and it appeared as though it was going to go well into the night. This type of event is one of those "pick your battles" situations. Was there weed being smoked? Yes. Was there booze being drank? Yes. Were we turning a blind eye to it? Yes.

The real problem of managing these types of gang events is balancing the nuisance against the patience of the poor residents of the neighborhood that don't want the nonsense going on in the first place. As the day turned to night the party continued to grow and get louder. There were well over one hundred people partying in the middle of the street. It was reaching a point where we would eventually have to intervene and shut down the event. When I say we I mean every cop in the entire precinct.

Eventually the command Officers for the precinct had enough of the neighbors calling 911 to complain so the order was given to gently move in and begin to disperse the crowd. Not being part of the Uniform Patrol Bureau meant that I had a different chain of command. The Gang Unit command had a much more hands-off approach to command, so those of us in the unit enjoyed much more autonomy and discretion. With that being said, I was always one to push the envelope regarding discretion. I readily admit that many times this led me to do reckless things that were not always well advised. This turned out to be one of those times.

I got a bright idea that it might be fun to sneak up on the party goers just to see what the reaction would be. To accomplish this, my partner and I parked well over a block away and began sneaking through the backyards towards the center of the party. Nobody else was in on the plan. It was just me and my partner. As we made our way through the last row of yards we could see the memorial site from our hiding spot between the houses. As we stood there watching I noticed one lone guy walking down the sidewalk in our direction. I could see his face and recognized him as one of the leaders of the Camden Block Crips. I also knew that he had just gotten out of prison from drug and gun charges.

When he got parallel to our hiding spot I called to him by name and stepped towards him from about twenty feet away. He didn't hesitate for even a split second; he took off running straight away from me. I of course gave chase, assuming he was running because he was carrying a gun. As you might imagine this drew attention from his fellow gang members in the crowd. It also drew attention from all the other cops since I was putting out the foot chase over the radio. I was starting to gain ground when out of the corner of my eye I saw my Sergeant running at us on an intercept course. Good, this would be over quickly. All of the sudden there was the sound of four or five gunshots from somewhere really close by.

I wasn't sure where the shots were coming from, and neither was my Sergeant because we both stopped running momentarily. We weren't the only ones that were confused. The guy we were chasing threw himself to the ground and started flailing. I thought to myself "what a strange reaction." Then it made sense. He thought we were shooting at him! The chase was now over because he just kept lying there on the ground. Me and my Sergeant made our way over there and cuffed him no problem. I re-traced the last twenty or so yards of the foot chase and found what I was looking for; a brown and black 9mm pistol in the grass. D.N.A. testing would later confirm that it was indeed dropped by the suspect during the chase.

The suspect ended up with a Federal Indictment for the gun charges and did about two and a half years in Federal prison. My Sergeant and I ended up with the unanswered question: who had been doing the shooting during the chase and were we the intended targets? It's one of those questions I'll never get an answer to.

GET SOME WOOD

During Field Training you get rotated to different parts of the city, and to different shifts. I was starting my first day with my new coach in the northeast precinct on the afternoon/evening shift. I was really excited. Every recruit looked forward to working northeast because that was where the action was. I found my coach and then together we made our way into the assembly room for roll-call. The Sergeant for the crew was a guy from an earlier story; the military guy with no sense of humor. It was obvious from the very start that he found recruits to be an annoyance. My very first roll call started out with a lecture by the Sarge as to what I would and would not be doing in his precinct. I thought to myself, just do what you're told, this phase will only last five weeks. At the end of his lecture for my edification he mandated that I needed to "get some wood." What he meant was, I needed to ditch the departmental issue collapsible baton and get one made of wood.

Great I thought, going old-school with the wooden baton. Only one problem; I had no idea where to get one. This is where having a coach comes into play. He told me where to go to get my baton. At first I didn't believe him, because I thought he was trying to pull a practical joke on me. As it turned out, he wasn't kidding.

On Leavenworth Street and Park Avenue there is a strip club. Behind the strip club the owner of the club had a woodshop. It gets even weirder. As legend has it the owner of the club, who is now deceased, was at one time the President of the Omaha chapter of the Hell's Angels Motorcycle Gang.

I did as I was instructed and made my way on my next day off to the shed behind the strip club. There I found an extremely weathered and mean looking man. Turned out he was a nice guy, just didn't have a lot to say. I introduced myself and told him who I was and why I was there. He had quite the woodshop in the little shed and I was impressed by the various creations he had strewn about. He directed me to the west wall of the shed and there hung about twenty different wood batons. It was at that point I got a lesson about the wood they were made from. The wood is called purpleheart and it comes from the rainforests of Brazil. It is among the densest and most weather resistant woods in the world.

It took me a long time to pick out my baton because they were all just really kick-ass cool. Finally I made my choice and paid my $40 bucks to the creator. I felt like I had just completed a rite of passage. On the next day back to work I proudly displayed my new baton for all to see. I was one step closer to becoming a real cop.

THAT'S HOW YOU CARRY A LITTLE FELON

This is another story for which I have to add the disclaimer I don't mean to offend any person or group of people. With that said, one of the more prominent gangs in Omaha is the 29th Street Bloods. Here's a fun fact about that gang. For the entire time I was on the Gang Unit one of the most feared members of that gang was....a dwarf. I'm dead serious. There was a kid in the gang that stood no taller than about four feet. I doubt he was even that tall. He was an odd looking kid because he had the hugest man-sized hands. Those hands were totally disproportional to the rest of his body. Those hands did however allow him to grasp a full sized pistol the same as a man twice his height. He was no stranger to guns; I think I caught him twice carrying a pistol.

One of my favorite memories regarding this little man came from a night we caught him in a stolen car. We knew exactly where he lived so we made a point of checking the house several times a day/night. On one such check we found a stolen Chevy Cavalier parked across the street from his house. My partner and I played a hunch that he would be driving the car at some point during our shift so we found a place to park and conduct surveillance. It took about two hours of sitting patiently, but finally our patience paid off. Little man and two of his siblings, also members of the gang, came out of the house and got into the stolen Chevy. Unbelievably little man was the one that was going to drive! I had no idea how he was going to manage driving that car.

This was exactly what we had hoped for; three gangbangers in a stolen car. The possibilities were intriguing. We had been conducting our surveillance from an unmarked car, so we had a marked cruiser assisting us to execute the traffic stop. As soon as they pulled away from the house we let the marked cruiser know that the target vehicle was on the move. They were only able to get about three blocks before the marked cruiser caught up to them. My partner and I were close on the rear bumper of the marked cruiser.

As soon as the cruiser got behind the target vehicle it turned immediately, heading down a side street. At that point the cruiser lit them up with the lights. To my dismay the car actually began to pull over. Damn! If they were pulling over that meant they weren't holding any weapons. Too bad, but at least we had them on the stolen car charge. To be on the safe side we decided to make the traffic stop a "high risk" stop, sometimes referred to as a "felony traffic stop." In a nutshell that means instead of going up to the stopped car, you call the occupants out at gunpoint and take them into custody one at a time under controlled conditions. This is done to insure the safety of all involved.

We started the process of removing the vehicle occupants. During this type of stop you typically start with the driver and have the person step out of the car while facing away from the cops. Then you have them take several steps backwards before having the person lie face down on the concrete. This is what we did with little man. Since it was my stop I nominated myself to be the one to take custody of little man. As soon as he was face down on the concrete I made my approach. I searched him to make sure he wasn't hiding a weapon, and then I cuffed him. I was kind of pissed off that we probably wouldn't find any guns in the car so the next thing I did was pretty unprofessional. For the amusement of all those at the scene I picked little man up by his belt and by the collar of his shirt, carrying him like a sack of potatoes back to the cruiser. I know I shouldn't have because it was unnecessarily demeaning. Looking back I don't feel too bad because let's be honest. You don't get many chances in life to carry a dwarf—especially a deviant gangbanging dwarf with a liking for gun violence.

WABBIT SEASON

This story takes place at "the circle." It was shortly after the inception of the tradition so there wasn't very many of us in attendance. The Sergeant had stopped for supplies earlier in the night at the downtown smoke shop. He had this fondness for these cheap little cigars called "Kentucky Cheroots." Pretty soon he had all of us hooked on them. So there we were smoking our smokes, talking about the events of the night. We tended to have our "circle meetings" on the last day of the workweek so we could stay out late. It was spring so it was a little chilly. To combat this we would often build a small bonfire, many times even cooking over the flame. The meetings were always so peaceful, truly medicine for the soul.

As a cop there are very few places you truly let your guard down and allow yourself to really relax. The circle was such a place; except for this night. We were all sitting around our bonfire enjoying the fellowship when the sound of gunfire rang out. We all went diving for the ground since most, if not all of us had left our guns in our cars! It took us several seconds to figure out what the hell was happening, and who was responsible. It turned out it was one of our own!

The cop who shall remain nameless had just gotten a new laser sight for his Glock, and apparently he had decided it was time to try it out. We all started screaming at him for scaring the piss out of us and demanded an explanation. It turned out the explanation was really simple. He had seen a rabbit and wanted to see if he could hit it with the help of his new laser sight. The answer was no. He did not hit the rabbit. He is given full credit for the new rule of the circle— **NO SHOOTING** at the circle!

FOOT CHASE...CHASE

It was about 100 degrees the day this strange foot chase took place. Me and my partner in the Gang Unit were patrolling the area of the 29th Street Bloods looking for gangbangers to mess with. As usual it took no time whatsoever for us to find our first candidates. It was a couple of the regulars, guys that we dealt with on an almost daily basis. Generally speaking they were the co-operative sort and understood we were all just playing a dangerous game. As we made approach in our Dodge Intrepid one of the guys started the textbook "fade" which is the prelude to a foot chase. The only way to deal with the "fade" is to get on your prey as quick as possible. My partner was driving that day which meant I was the chaser of all runners. That's traditionally the best way to orchestrate a foot chase; one cop on foot and one driving parallel in the cruiser.

As we got close the "fade" turned into a dead sprint. We had anticipated this so I was out the car door quickly and chasing my guy. I loved foot chases, but chasing guys in 100 degree heat saps your energy incredibly quickly. My runner had a pretty big head start on me so my goal was to keep him in sight to see if he would throw any drugs or guns. I don't know if I mentioned it before; any time you put a foot chase out over the police radio you get every Officer in the precinct coming to help. This is why it's so important to at least keep your suspect in sight throughout the chase.

The chase was going pretty routinely until something behind me caught my attention. To my utter astonishment the other guy from the start of this incident was chasing ME as I chased his buddy. This was a new one! I had never been chased during a foot chase before. It was pretty unnerving because I didn't know why. I didn't know if his plan was distraction so his buddy could get away, or if he wanted to shoot me in the back. Thankfully the guy I was chasing was fading fast and I was gaining on him. I made it to within about twenty yards of him when all of the sudden my partner appeared in the cruiser and damn near ran the suspect over. Not being very smart he gave up right in the middle of the street on the scalding hot pavement. So, that's where he got cuffed…slowly.

By the time I had the suspect cuffed and secured in the cruiser the other guy that was chasing me was nowhere to be found. Now I had to go find him. It didn't take long before I found him loitering by a school playground. There were several cruisers around so the first thing I had to do was make sure that nobody had their cruiser cameras turned on. The newer digital cameras would automatically start recording once the lights and sirens were activated so you had to be careful to turn the cameras off manually. With that done I proceeded to threaten the guy that had chased me with every threat I could think of, most of which involved bodily injury to him. I also decided that he was going to get a criminal citation for "Obstructing the Administration of Law." The charge was ultimately dismissed, but I'm sure the object lesson stuck. Don't ever chase a cop.

LISTEN TO YOUR MOMMA

Working in the Criminal Investigations Bureau had some great benefits. Lots of free time, set your own pace, long lunches, etc. It also had a few drawbacks, the biggest of which was the rotating weekend duty. There always had to be two Detectives working Saturday and Sunday at Central Headquarters to meet with the Deputy County Attorney for the bond settings with the duty judge over the phone. After that was done the day could go easy or it could go hard, depending if any serious crimes happened during the day.

I remember it was a Sunday morning and I was on weekend duty. It was early like 10:30 or 11:00. I was monitoring the radio on scan mode so I could listen to all four precincts at once, hoping nothing big would happen. No such luck. Alert tones went out indicating that a priority one call was about to be dispatched. It turned out to be a shooting down in the northeast precinct. I didn't gear up and leave the building just yet. I wanted to make sure it was a legitimate shooting that would require my presence. So I waited for the initial responding patrol Officers to get on scene and assess the situation.

The victim had taken several hits to the leg and side through the driver's door of his Chevy Suburban. He initially gave up who he thought the shooter was because I think he thought he was going to die. The squad got him stabilized and to the hospital, at which point he became uncooperative. This was fairly common amongst gangbangers, the whole philosophy of staying silent and not talking to the police. I decided not to go to the shooting scene. I decided my time was better spent trying to identify the shooter via several police databases on the computer. In about an hour I was pretty sure I had the shooter identified. After that I produced a photo line-up including my suspected shooter. With line-up in hand I jumped in a car and headed for the hospital.

I found my victim on a gurney in one of the trauma bays. He was waiting for the radiologist and the surgeon to read his x-rays. He was suffering in silence but I could tell he was in a lot of pain. He was an O.G. (Original Gangster) from before my time, but somebody obviously still had an axe to grind with him. I walked up to him and introduced myself. In return I got a stare of indignation. I could see this was going to go as I had figured. I started talking anyway, if for no other reason than to say I had tried. I explained to him that I had a photo line-up that I wanted to show him. To put it nicely he told me to pound sand. I was about to speak my peace to him and leave when all of the sudden his mother walked into the trauma bay. Unbeknownst to me, she had been in the vehicle when it got shot up. My victim had apparently been driving his mother around that Sunday morning.

She walked straight up to the gurney and asked me "Who the hell are you?" I explained who I was and why I was there. I further explained that her son was not helping my investigation. That was all it took. She laid into her son, who was about thirty years old, and let him have it good. By the time she was done I had a completed photo line-up, with the correct suspect identified. It took me about two more hours and I had my Felony Arrest Warrant written and ready for the judge's signature.

The Fugitive Unit found the suspect a couple days later. He ended up getting sentenced to nine years in prison. I didn't get a thank you from one person.

WORST CALL EVER

This next story is a hard one for me to write because it was so traumatic. It happened during my first year out on my own. It came out as a "Child Neglect" call and I was dispatched to a hospital emergency room. I hated these calls. I hated seeing the evil that happens to innocent children. Nothing could have prepared me for what I was going to see at the hospital. I walked in and located the E.R. bay where the victim was located. Inside were the doctor and a small boy about 2 years old. He had a sheet over the lower half of his little body and he was eerily calm. I asked the doctor why I had been dispatched and he stated it would be best to just show me.

The doctor pulled the sheet down and I about vomited. The injury to this poor little boy was horrific. The doctor explained that the family pet, a pit-bull, had bitten off and eaten the little boy's genitalia. I can't put into words my emotions when I saw the little boy's injury. I did know that the ensuing investigation would be beyond my level of investigation. I called the Child Victim Unit of the department and spoke with one of the Detectives. The Detective asked that I detain any of the child's family that was present at the hospital, which I did.

The Detective made record time getting to the hospital. After receiving a briefing by the E.R. doctor the Detective called the Humane Society to have the suspect pit-bull impounded. He then asked me to show him who was there from the family. I showed him to the only person I had found, the mother's boyfriend. Other Detectives from the unit had gone to the residence to secure what was now a crime scene.

The Detective with me at the hospital asked me if I would sit in on the interview with the mother's boyfriend. I was feeling pretty angry at that point so I of course wanted to hear what this guy had to say. Without going into too many details, the story was the dog "didn't mean to do it, he was just trying to bite the dirty diaper on the child." How's that for an excuse for the wounded child laying in the nearby hospital bed? I was getting madder by the minute and I could tell the Detective was as well. At some point during the interview the guy asked what was going to happen to the dog. I thought to myself really? Wouldn't it be a little more important to find out what was going to happen to the child? At that point the Detective let the guy have the truth, none too kindly. The dog was being euthanized in an attempt to recover any part of the little boy's genitalia. The guy broke down crying. I thought to myself how sad, because I knew the guy was crying for the dog not the little boy. That story will stay with me forever.

CRACK WAVE

Before I started in the Gang Unit there was a Detective in the unit who had legendary status. I wish I could use his name but I can't. He was feared throughout the criminal community for his sixth-sense and relentless pursuit of crime. He retired shortly before I did, but his legend still lived on for at least six months after he retired. The criminals thought he was somehow hiding from sight but still doing the job. It became comical after a while. In any event this story always makes me smile.

I was riding around the northeast precinct late in the afternoon with my partner for that day. We were doing nothing in particular, just enjoying the warm afternoon. As we were driving we got flagged down by the legend. He was riding around by himself in an old red Dodge Ram pickup that was one of the unit's undercover vehicles. He directed us into a nearby church parking lot so he could talk to us. As usual he was short on conversation and straight to the point. He told us he needed our help, to which we were happy to oblige. He went on to tell us this: "There's a guy standing around the corner two blocks down—he's going to have crack on him." He further explained he wanted us to make the contact so he didn't blow his cover and burn his undercover vehicle. That made perfect sense, but I had to ask; "How do you know he has crack on him?" With a deadpan expression he replied simply "He waved at me."

Not convinced, but trusting the legend, we went in search of the alleged suspect. We found him standing on the corner right where he was supposed to be. Luckily he was drinking from an open container of alcohol so we immediately placed him under arrest. As I searched him I found several small "twenty-piece" baggies of packaged crack-cocaine in the watch pocket of his jeans. The legend had been spot on. The guy was selling crack from the street corner, and all he needed was a wave of the hand to know it. He hit us up on the radio and told us to go book the suspect downtown and that he would be down at some point to do the paperwork. That is how legends do it my friends. From that point forward that would be the standard I tried to achieve.

TAKE THAT CHAMP

The time spent in the training academy as a recruit seemed to take forever. There were so many things we had to learn, and most of it was academic in nature. I hated the classroom work, so I relished the days we did activities that were physical in nature. Towards the end of the academy it gets physical really quickly. One of the last units to complete is mock scenarios, also called red-man drills due to the red pads worn by the instructors. The red-man drills are the culmination of all the instruction over the course of the academy. Essentially they are arrest scenarios, where as the recruit you are required to physically arrest an uncooperative subject.

The red pads worn by the instructors are there to protect them because the scenarios get VERY physical. That of course is the objective of the drill—to gauge how a recruit will likely react on the street. To make the scenarios as tough as possible, the instructors were hand-picked from the toughest of all the cops on the department. Hardly fair I thought, but oh well, it would make for good training.

Let me define "tough" for clarification purposes. The guy I had to fight was a professional U.F.C. fighter and titleholder. In other words the toughest guy you'd ever meet. The fight I had with him took place nearly fourteen years ago, but I remember it like it was yesterday. Extreme fear tends to burn the memories into your mind.

The fight scenarios all took place in a gymnasium on wrestling mats to minimize the risk of injury to all involved. Mine started with a briefing by two academy instructors—I had to arrest a drunken guy outside of a bar. I was required to follow all the proper police procedures and pretend it was a real 911 call. So there I stood in my blue recruit uniform with a fake gun belt, baton, and police radio. All I had to do was subdue a U.F.C. champion fighter. I was trembling as the mock scenario started but I tried to hide it since we were being graded.

I remember approaching the instructor and initially trying to gain compliance through verbal measures. These were of course meant to fail so that going "hands-on" would be inevitable. Finally, after long debate I made my move trying to reach in and catch the instructor by surprise. Before I knew what had happened I found myself on my hands and knees with the instructor behind me. At that point the human instinct of self preservation took over. I vaguely remember throwing a vicious right elbow backwards to no avail. I'm pretty sure we weren't supposed to throw elbows but at that point I was trying to survive.

The instructor toyed with me for several minutes as a cat does with a mouse. Finally, two more recruits were added into the fight and the three of us then tried to get the instructor into handcuffs. It was still to no avail—the man was a machine. At long last he played along with the scenario and let us handcuff him. It had only been three minutes long, but it had felt like an hour had gone by. I was exhausted.

After all the recruits had completed the scenarios we had a group de-briefing with all the instructors. To my amazement, my earlier elbow throw had given the champ a nice black eye. He was grinning as he complimented me on the strike. I didn't know whether to say thank you, or "I'm really sorry." I don't remember if I said anything. I was in awe of such a man that seemed to feel no pain. Make no mistake however; I'm proud of the fact that I gave a U.F.C. champion a black eye, even if by accident.

SERIOUS HANDCUFFING VIOLATION

In 2003 my Army Reserve unit was called up to active duty for deployment in support of Operation Iraqi Freedom. When I got back in 2004 I got stuck working southwest Omaha, the place where the old cops go to retire on duty. I got stuck there because I had come back between the semi-annual bid boards where you bid for your spot based upon your seniority. So I was stuck for like four months until the next bid board. I tried to make the best of it. I was glad to be back on American soil and back to my police career so I was full of piss and vinegar. I was the only one on my crew with such an attitude. As a matter of fact they all got tired of me rousing up trouble on a daily basis. I didn't care I was having fun.

One afternoon right after roll call I had made my way down to a subdivision called the "Karen Hood." It was one of the few spots in the entire southwest precinct where serious crime could be found. There was a gang of hoodlum teenagers, burglaries, car thefts, and of course methamphetamine use—just my kind of area to find something to do. It didn't take long. I was rolling through the hood when I saw a parked car on the street, occupied by two dirt-balls that looked up to no good. As soon as they saw my cruiser they pulled into the nearest driveway and got out of the car. Then they went to the front door of the residence and started knocking. I had seen this trick before and wasn't falling for it. I pulled into the driveway behind their car and blocked them. As I approached them I could see open containers of beer in the center console of the car. Super, I would write them both tickets for open containers. As I got closer one guy bolted around the back of the house, and the other one I quickly snatched. He had a long sleeved flannel shirt on and when I went to cuff him I realized he had a cast on his left arm.

Crap, they didn't teach us how to deal with this in the academy, especially when you've got a second guy running from you. So, I improvised, I snapped the cuff on his right wrist and drug him over to the front of my cruiser. I placed the left handcuff around the push-bar of my car and took off after his partner. These guys were in their forties and obviously out of shape because I actually managed to catch the other guy as well. When I got back to my cruiser I found the first suspect right where I left him, except now he had company. One of the older crusty cops from the crew had actually made the effort to come help me. He didn't say much other than to not get caught cuffing guys to the push-bars of cruisers. I thanked him for the wisdom and wrote my two suspects their tickets.

THE STEAMING GUN

This story happened towards the end of my career, somewhere around the Christmas holiday in 2010. I was still in the gang unit. The partner and I were killing time before the end of our shift when all of the sudden two other Gang Unit Detectives jumped on the radio yelling "shots-fired, shots-fired." Judging by the stress in their voices they were awfully close to the shots. After a bit they were back on the radio putting out an address for a shooting scene. They were also advising the suspect(s) were in the area on foot. As with any shooting every cop in the precinct was making best speed to the scene.

My partner and I were close so we got there fairly quickly. The other two gang Detectives had already found a dead guy on the front porch of a house. People were screaming everywhere. Some were from the house where the dead guy was, some were neighbors, cops were screaming at people: general chaos. Cops and cruisers were showing up and parking everywhere, not to mention the fire department and ambulance. It looked like a Christmas tree with all the lights from the vehicles rotating and flashing.

I remember it was cold that night, and all of the sudden I had an epiphany. The police helicopter Able-One was flying that night and was hovering overhead using their searchlight to look for any suspects fleeing on foot. I got on the radio and made a suggestion to the spotter. I told them to turn off their searchlight and switch to their F.L.I.R.—Forward Looking Infra-Red camera system. The F.L.I.R. is usually used to look for individuals trying to hide through detection of their heat signature. My idea was to use the same principle, but to look for a weapon instead of a person. I reasoned that a firearm that had just been fired would be warm enough to stand out given the cold conditions that night.

  The helicopter performed the switch and it only took about thirty seconds for them to find the heat signature of a handgun. They were able to direct me to the exact spot where it was lying in the grass between the sidewalk and the street, directly across from the house with the dead guy. Ironically, there were three cruisers parked right next to it, and probably half a dozen cops had likely walked right past the firearm. I don't remember if it turned out to be the murder weapon or not. None-the-less it became a great reminder that technology can be a wonderful thing sometimes.

CARROTS IN THE DRESSER

There was a guy way down in northeast Omaha. He was a legendary criminal and testimony to the revolving door of justice. He was a huge crank addict and was always stealing something, driving a stolen car, or had outstanding arrest warrants. He was also a lot of fun because he never gave up without a chase. It was assumed, and he made it clear to every cop he met; you would have to catch him. He lived with his mom whenever he wasn't out living on the streets. Every cop knew where his mom lived. I felt bad for the lady because she was genuinely nice, and her son brought a lot of drama to her house.

One particular night I saw him getting out of a parked car near his mother's house that happened to be stolen. The chase was on! He ran straight for his mother's house with me on his heels. He was always a tough rundown because he was deceptively fast. He made it around the back of his mother's house....and he was gone. Cops were showing up to establish a perimeter but he was nowhere to be found outside. We knocked on the door and his mother let us search inside the house. I couldn't believe how he had simply vanished into thin air.

I ended up getting an arrest warrant for him so that I could chase him again next time I saw him. It didn't take more than a week and I saw him standing in his mother's front yard. I went screaming up the driveway with my cruiser and almost ran him over. He JUMPED the hood of my car as I screeched to a stop about six inches from his mom's mailbox. Around the back of the house he went me on his heels, and poof! He was gone again! I could not believe it! We went through the same routine, set up the perimeter, search the inside of the house; same result. This time around we had even used a K-9 search dog on the inside of the house—nothing. He had now become my mission. I could think of nothing else other than catching this shape-shifter!

I got my chance another couple of weeks later. It all pretty much went down the same way as the last two times, except this time I had literally been on his heels as he went around the house. This time I was sure he was in that house. By now, I was getting called the "cop who cried wolf" since I couldn't corner this guy. My patrol Sergeant showed up and asked me how sure I was about him being in the house. I told him 100%. So, my Sergeant called for a K-9. It was a different dog that showed up from the time before. Into the house we went. We were doing a systematic room by room search when we entered one of the back bedrooms of the house. Immediately the K-9 went crazy, barking and snarling at a dresser. I cannot tell you how surprised we all were when the dresser started talking to us saying "I give up!"

The K-9 handler secured his dog and we pulled the dresser from the wall. There was my guy, eating baby carrots from a Ziploc baggie. The creative bastard had hollowed out a standard dresser and glued the fronts of the drawers back on to make it look normal. He surrendered without incident and I took him to jail. I asked him on the way down because I had to know; had he been in the same dresser on the other occasions? He just grinned at me in the rear view mirror and said "Yep."

LISTEN, I'VE GOT WEED

There were a few times during my career when I heard something that made me go hmmmm. Me and my long time partner on the Gang Unit got lots of tidbits of information on gangbangers from lots of different sources. Sometimes it was ordinary citizens, other times it was a disgruntled girlfriend, still other times it was from guys trading their own freedom for information. No matter the source, sometimes the information was good, sometimes it was bad.

We had information from several different sources about one guy that was moving a lot of various drugs. With so many sources we decided we should make this guy a priority target. We did our research and studied our target, where he lived, what he drove, etc. After that we started hunting. One afternoon we saw him pulling away from a recording studio. We had the unmarked Dodge Intrepid so we were able to sneak up behind him. We weren't even that close when we could smell the weed coming from his car like a wake behind a boat. It was obvious he was smoking as he drove. We lit him up and made our initial approach. The first words out of his mouth were "Listen, I've got weed." We told him we weren't surprised since we could smell it all the way back at our car. Still, that seemed odd that those would be his first words. Something wasn't right.

He voluntarily handed over his bag of weed which was almost a full quart sized Ziploc bag. I had my partner entertain the suspect in conversation while I called our Lieutenant. I told him we had info from several sources on this guy, in addition to his erratic behavior on our stop. Our Lieutenant gave us what I was hoping for; permission to strip search our suspect. I told my partner our good news, so my partner cuffed our suspect and put him in our car. I jumped in the suspect's car and we all drove to the northeast precinct building for the strip search.

We hadn't told our suspect the plan but we could tell he was getting really nervous. This convinced us even further that we were on the right path of investigation.

We took our suspect into one of the precinct interview rooms and we could see the look of defeat in his eyes. We had him. When we got down to the underwear it was plainly obvious he was hiding a big bag—no pun intended. The bag turned out to contain over two hundred ecstasy pills. Needless to say we were delighted, and he was not. Lesson learned: People don't give up that easy unless they're hiding something.

TRASH CAN SKS

This is a story about the Victor Street Bloods. For background sake the Victor Street Bloods are a third generation street gang in Omaha. They started out when crack-cocaine was hitting big in Omaha in the late 80's and early 90's. As many gangs do, they took their name from the street on which they operated—Victor Street. The street itself is only two blocks long, but as gang history goes you'll never find a more storied street.

As I mentioned, gang life was the way of life on Victor Street up until I left the gang unit in 2011. I don't know about today, but I suspect little has changed. We made Victor Street one of our favorite patrol areas because there was ALWAYS at least one gangbanger just hanging out somewhere along the street. There were also lots of interesting abandoned houses on the street which we would occasionally walk through, sometimes finding hidden treasures of contraband.

The bangers on Victor Street were so used to seeing us that most of the time they just ignored the fact that we were there walking amongst them. They were a very disciplined lot for the most part, and would only run when they had a pistol on them. That was the telltale sign for us. If they were running they were holding. Case in point—my partner and I were making our first trip of the night down Victor Street when we saw about six guys standing in the driveway of our particular favorite hang-out house. As we rolled up they were all just like statues. We stopped the car and got out; nobody moved. This was odd even for this group of individuals. Then I saw it: sticking barrel down in a trash can on the side of the house was a very nice **SKS** assault rifle. It was loaded of course. An assault rifle in the trash can ready to go, that would explain the strange behavior. I grabbed the rifle after putting rubber gloves on. Maybe we would get lucky and the crime lab would lift a print off of the weapon. Nobody moved an inch or said a word the entire time I handled the rifle, before securing it in our trunk. I don't even think my partner and I exchanged any banter prior to leaving for Central Headquarters to book the rifle into evidence.

The crime lab did not get any prints off the rifle. At the end of the day all we had was a nice assault rifle labeled "found property." Yet another firearm destined to be melted down. A lot of days were like that in the Gang Unit; taking guns off the streets with no suspect to show for it. Just another day on Victor Street.

THANK GOD FOR THE SECOND CRUISER

Real cops follow a "code" when it comes to safety. The first rule of police work is everyone goes home safe at the end of the shift. To accomplish this you have to work as a team. In certain precincts in Omaha this rule is alive and well. If you stop a car, then other cops will drive by to check on you. If you get in a chase, the other cops in the precinct will bust their asses to come and help. It's the code. I've seen it, lived it, and most likely been saved by it.

Working northeast one night we stopped a car late in the area referred to as Murdertown. The driver acted strangely from the start. Instead of pulling over to the curb on the street he intentionally pulled into a parking lot. As was our habit we had both the cruiser's spotlights aimed into the suspect car to blind the driver and cover our approach. I wasn't sure, but I didn't think the driver ever put the car in park even though he was stopped. He kept looking over his shoulder even though he was looking into spotlights. Just as we were getting ready to exit our cruiser a second cruiser pulled up next to us and added their spotlights to ours. The driver of the car about broke his own neck looking to see who had just pulled up. As soon as he realized it was more cops he took off and the car chase was on.

It became clear right away that this guy had ties to Murdertown by the way he kept circling the same four to six blocks in a figure eight pattern. I know I've said before most car chases end in foot chases. This guy was obviously waiting for his spot and opportunity to bail on foot. Eventually after going around in circles for two long minutes he took a back alley between two streets. He was a fast guy and got away clean. We didn't have a perimeter or anything set up. By the time we got out of our cruisers he was probably already inside a house watching us. He abandoned the car which was unlicensed. The lack of license plates was the reason we stopped it in the first place.

I made my way to the now empty car and there on the front bench seat of the old piece of crap Olds Cutlass was a sawed-off double barreled shotgun with a pistol grip. When I inspected it I found both barrels were loaded. As I stood there re-playing what had just happened I started to get a chill up my spine. I'm convinced that had the second cruiser not shown up I, or my partner might have become a statistic. I believe that driver had every intention of emptying both barrels at the first cop that reached his window. We never did figure out who the guy was.

17 ROUND MIRACLE

One premise I've come to accept is this: If it's not your time, it's not your time. I've lived it several times and I've witnessed it many more. None of the times compare to what I call the "17 round miracle." It happened during my time on the Gang Unit. We were having a hard time finding any good action in northeast Omaha, so we went hunting further west in some of the spots we knew the bangers liked to go when they wanted to lay low. We were on Ames Avenue at about 65th Street when all of the sudden we heard a ton of gunshots going off in rapid succession...and they were real close. We heard squealing tires exactly one block to our south so we rounded the next corner as fast as we could hoping to get a glimpse of a fleeing car. No such luck, the car squealing tires was gone.

We did the next thing on the gunshot checklist; we started looking for a victim. What we found was the "17 round miracle." We found a guy sitting on the curb staring blankly into space. At first I assumed he had been shot so we hurried to get out and talk to him. He wasn't shot, he was in shock. We asked him if he was alright and he just pointed to a parked car along the curb next to where he was sitting. Then we saw it plain as day—the car had bullet holes all along the driver's side. Seventeen bullet holes to be exact. In the street next to the car were seventeen spent shell casings.

I asked him if he had been inside the car when it was shot up. He just nodded in the affirmative. I sat down on the curb next to him and eventually he started to come back to reality. I told him I was taking him to Vegas because he was the luckiest man I had ever seen! He looked at me and nodded again. After about twenty minutes of just sitting and talking to the guy he finally regained his composure enough to tell us what happened. He said he was just sitting in the car listening to music when a car pulled up next to him and started "blasting." He didn't get a look at the shooter or the car because he said he was too busy ducking.

I went over and looked at the car again because I couldn't believe he had truly been inside during the shooting. It just seemed to bend the laws of physics. Then a witness wandered over and confirmed the guy had indeed been inside as he claimed. I called a crime lab technician to the scene to collect the shell casings, and more importantly take pictures of the car. This was truly something that had to be seen to be believed. It wasn't that guy's time.

THAT'S NOT PANCAKE MIX

It was 2005 and I had recently been promoted to the Criminal Investigations Bureau—AKA Detective Bureau. The Bureau was divided into units, and I worked on the North Investigations Unit. There were four of us plus a Sergeant. Somehow we got roped into working an investigation with the Special Investigations Unit from Offutt Air force Base. It was a case involving a ton of merchandise being stolen off the loading dock at the Base Exchange store before ever making it to the store shelves. They got wise to the operation by auditing the shipping manifests to what they counted on the shelves. They reviewed the back dock surveillance camera footage, and just like that they had their suspect. That's how my unit got involved; the guy responsible lived in north Omaha and just worked on base. So really it was a jurisdictional issue when it came time to write the search warrant for the house.

As search warrant affidavits go it was easy to write. The only sticky point was that the target suspect had a weapons history. Because of his history we were required by policy to use the S.W.A.T. Team. The more people involved the more complicated the logistics. I ended up sitting in the back of a beat up old van conducting surveillance prior to the arrival of the S.W.A.T. Team. There was nothing I hated more than surveillance. I just couldn't stand the boredom. At long last the S.W.A.T. Team pulled up with the rest of my unit in tow.

    The front door got kicked and it didn't take long for the team to secure the occupants in the house. It turned out there were a couple of little kids inside so the first job was to get a grandparent over to the house to pick the kids up. No sense traumatizing them any more than they already had been by the means of our entry. The next step was to get the S.W.A.T. Team out of the way so we could start our search. They were all too happy to oblige now that their work was done. As they were getting ready to leave one of the S.W.A.T. members pulled me aside and said "You better check the stove." I told him I would and that was that. After a while I made my way into the kitchen and remembered that I was supposed to check the stove. At first glance it looked fine to me. There was a big silver mixing bowl sitting on top of the stove and it looked like somebody was cooking something with flour; maybe pancakes or some baked goods. Then it dawned on me. Somebody was about to cook alright and the main ingredient was powder cocaine! I don't remember how much it ended up weighing, but I can tell you it would have yielded a good amount of crack-cocaine by the time it was finished.

When it was all said and done we had truckloads full of T.V.'s, DVD players, and all sorts of brand new merchandise that never made it into the base store. The suspect never admitted to anything. In fact, all the theft charges were ultimately dismissed pursuant to the Federal Indictment on the drug charges. The case served as a good reminder. You never know what you're going to find when you kick someone's front door in.

4ᵀᴴ OF JULY FAMILY BONDING

Much like New Year's Eve, the 4th of July was an excuse for everyone to shoot off their guns without much chance of police intervention. With all the fireworks going off it just becomes one huge event of sensory overload. Trying to distinguish the fireworks from the gunfire all night used to give me a huge headache. As a matter of fact, the 4th of July is forever ruined for me.

I was on the Gang Unit during the time frame of this story, so we were working all day and night as usual for this particular holiday. We were assisting the Uniform Patrol units breaking up a huge house party, when the sound of gunfire rang out from about four houses down the street. Not just any gunfire, it was the unmistakable sound of an AK-47 letting loose. Just like any other time I was the moth to the flame when I heard the shots going off. I tore off across the street in the direction I estimated the shots originated from. Luckily one other cop had followed me. It didn't take us long to find the house because another salvo of fire erupted as we approached.

We waited for the shooting to stop and then like ninjas we jumped through a hedgerow and began yelling at everyone with our guns drawn. I was appalled by what we had stumbled into. It was of course celebratory gunfire, but that wasn't what pissed me off. Sitting in a lawn chair was a woman about eighty years old, obviously a Grandmother or Great Grandmother. In her lap was a toddler, sound asleep wearing nothing but a diaper. I came unglued. For starters I didn't know how that little child had managed to sleep through what was happening. More importantly, I had to know the answer to the hundred dollar question: Who the hell thinks this scene was anywhere close to being acceptable? I made the old woman take the child inside to bed and then I proceeded to chew the ass of the gun owner for twenty minutes straight.

I could tell after about the first ten minutes of my rant that my insights were falling upon deaf ears. I didn't care. It was more for my benefit anyway. The only thing the gun owner wanted to know was whether or not I was going to take his guns? He explained the rifle and the shotgun we found were brand new and he had just spent $800 buying them. I don't think I answered him as I handed him his ticket and confiscated his weapons.

I remember the day of the court proceedings. I made a specific point to talk to the City Prosecutor with my feelings on the case. I told him I didn't care what the suspect got for a penalty as long as the weapons were ordered by the judge to be destroyed. The suspect got a fine, and I got my wish. I guess justice was served.

VIDEO FOOTAGE OF HIS FAVORITE COP

Earlier in the book I told the story of the house the Gang Unit raided on New Year's Eve. What I failed to mention was that house was one of the strongholds for a gang called the 37th Street Crips. During my five years in the Gang Unit they were one of the most active gangs around. Of particular note; they tended to be one of the most shot at gangs. Because of that fact our unit had a very heavy presence in their area of operation. This was helped by the fact that their "turf" was geographically very close to the precinct building. I would venture a guess during the summer months we would drive through the 37th Street area no less than five or six times a shift, sometimes maybe as many as ten times.

It was the following spring after serving the New Year's Eve search warrant when a funny tradition started. One of the residents from the house we raided had taken a flattering, but paranoid liking to me. Every time we made a pass through the 37th Street area we made a point to go past his house. One day during one of our passes we observed this particular individual sitting on his retaining wall holding a video camera. As we drove by he yelled "Robocop!" I didn't think anything of it since this guy was kind of strange anyway. I figured all the drugs had finally taken their toll on the guy.

    The next day we were driving by again, and he was in the exact same spot with his video camera. He yelled "Robocop!" as we passed. Two days in a row, that was a little odd I thought. The next day same sequence of events as the previous two days. ThIs was now bordering on obsessive. This behavior went on for an entire month before I finally stopped to ask him what the hell he was doing. I also asked if he was really recording me. He showed me that he was actually recording. He didn't give me the reason why. This went on for an entire summer. After a while I just accepted and ignored his erratic behavior.

    Flash forward to the next spring. The video camera was gone, but he still loved to shout "Robocop" from his perch on the retaining wall. I have no idea what he did with all the video footage. What I do know is that none of it ever ended up with the Internal Affairs Unit.

BLIZZARD BURGLAR

I was in the Field Training Program straight out of the academy working during a nasty, nasty blizzard. This was the phase when I was working with the coach that liked to sleep whenever possible. He was happy to see the snow because he was thinking it would be a great night to catch up on his sleep. The roads were a mess, and the rear wheel drive Ford Crown Victoria cruisers didn't do too well in the wet stuff. As a matter of fact our Sergeant had made it a point to tell us in roll call to stay off the roads if possible.

We had just left the assembly building and made it to a nearby hole when alert tones went out for a burglary in progress to a business. Maybe we had been wrong about the expected lack of crime for the night. The business wasn't too far from where we were parked so we decided to go to the call with the Officers that were dispatched. My coach told me if he had to be awake, then he was going to make me learn something. We made pretty good time to the business which turned out to be a jewelry store. It was a straight up "smash and grab." The burglar had thrown a concrete cinder block through the plate glass store front. Once inside he had most likely used a hammer to smash into the individual display cases.

We started looking around the front of the business and quickly found footprints leading to and from the point of entry. As we followed the prints around to the rear of the building we discovered a different set of prints; tire tracks from a four-wheeler. It was snowing hard, but not hard enough to completely cover the tracks if we hurried. So, my coach and I volunteered to follow the tracks. It was really pretty easy. There had been almost zero vehicle traffic except for the snowplows and other cop cars, so four-wheeler tracks were easily discernible.

As we followed the tracks we could see the faint remains of the four-wheeler path on the way to the business. It was clear the burglar had a plan. There was no meandering through the neighborhoods or wasted driving. The path away from the business followed the same route the burglar had taken to the business. It didn't take long before our hunt ended at a garage door to a residence. My coach put out the address of our suspect house and asked for more cops to come to our location. He then told me to grab the Polaroid camera and snap a quick picture of the tracks leading into the garage. Then came the crappy part; my coach and I had to go and stand on opposing corners of the house to make sure nobody left the house. By standing on opposing corners two Officers can watch all four sides of a building, thereby securing it.

Thankfully we didn't have to wait very long before the other cops started showing up. Lucky for us the lady of the house signed a "permission to search" form which saved us from having to write a search warrant. Truth be told it was almost as if she wanted us to get her boyfriend out of her life. He of course played dumb the entire time. We found the still hot four-wheeler in the garage, parked in a pool of melted snow. Not only did we find the get-a-way vehicle, we found enough stolen crap to fill a small pawn shop. Yes, we found a bunch of jewelry too.

TOO MUCH PEPPER

This story is one that always makes me smile, no matter how many times I think about it. It's a story from Hank's Place, the bar where I worked off-duty with my good friend. It was summer, and it was a scorching hot night. Not only was it hot out, it was humid. Unfortunately, the off-duty policy dictated that cops working at bars were not allowed to work inside the bar. That left us to stand and sweat outside in the doorway. No matter, we were getting paid well so no sense in complaining.

It was nearing 1:00 A.M., the time we helped the bar owner Hank clear everybody out and towards their cars. The first of the patrons were just starting to reach the doorway as a massive brawl erupted inside. I took a quick peek inside and saw that it was going to be messy and nasty. Bodies and furniture were flying everywhere and people were struggling to reach the front door. I was pondering what our move should be when my buddy very calmly looked over at me and said "Watch this. It'll be over in thirty seconds." Apparently my buddy knew something I didn't.

It wasn't so much that he knew something I didn't; he just had a lot more time on the job than

I did. Experience truly is the greatest teacher. My buddy took his pepper spray from the holder on his duty belt and held it as high as he could above his head. He then proceeded to empty an entire can of pepper spray into the inlet of the air conditioner unit mounted above the front door. Then he looked at me and simply said "Step back." His tactic was pure genius. The air conditioner turned the stream of pepper spray into a fog which was then blown throughout the inside of the entire bar.

Thirty seconds was a pretty close guess. People came flooding out the front door coughing, crying, rubbing their eyes, dripping snot, and generally cussing the police. The smell of pepper was enough to make a person gag, and many people were. It didn't take long and the bar was empty save for one person. The last person to walk out the bar door was the owner Hank. He didn't thank us for saving his furniture like I thought he should. He just looked at us with tears in his eyes and coughed the words—"Please don't ever do that again."

DIRECTIONS FROM A CONCERNED CITIZEN

I was riding with my last partner on the Gang Unit. We had information about a particularly nasty member of the gang the Hilltop Crips. Our information was that a girlfriend had been renting him cars to drive and he had been responsible for a ton of recent "shots-fired" calls. We were told that he didn't roll anywhere without a "strap." That is to say he carried a gun with him wherever he went. Being the adrenaline junkie I was anxious to run across this guy. I know that sounds crazy, but that was my mentality at that point in my life.

I distinctly remember it was a Sunday when we ran across him. I know it was a Sunday because there was the traditional gathering of people at Carter Park for Sunday BBQ and picnics. We actually ran across him twice that day. The first time he smoked us and got away almost immediately. It was obvious our target had no intention of letting us stop him. He was driving a brand new Dodge Charger; a favorite rental car for gangbangers. Our five year old Dodge Intrepid was no match for his Charger, but I had confidence in my driving skills if we got close enough. The only question was how crazy was this guy going to get?

The second time we came across him was inside Carter Park where everyone was enjoying the day with their families. This was definitely not the setting to get in a police chase or a shootout. He saw us coming almost as soon as we saw him. He took off through the park, driving over the grass and around scared people. Okay, he was going to be crazy. We let him get out of the park before we made our intention clear to chase him. As soon as we were clear of the families it was game on! I told my partner to stay off the radio; we were going to do this one "silent and deep." I knew there was no way in hell that the precinct command would allow a pursuit in the middle of a Sunday afternoon.

After a couple of minutes of chasing this guy I had a moment of clarity. I knew how we were going to put this out on the radio without saying we were chasing a car. I grabbed the microphone and told the dispatcher "we were told by a concerned citizen about a reckless driver in the area....." I then went on to give out our direction of travel and the vehicle description, just like you would do in a pursuit. Two things were now working in our favor. The other cops in the precinct knew what I was up to. So did command for that matter, but I had an ace in-the-hole. Gang Unit cars were not equipped with cameras so as long as nothing catastrophic occurred we had plausible deniability.

I pulled the same trick several more times as we continued to chase our suspect, citing updates from more "concerned citizens." I don't know exactly how long we chased that Dodge Charger, but it was a good long while. Finally we lost him; we just didn't have the horsepower to keep up forever. About an hour after the "chase" ended one of the Uniform Patrol Officers found the Charger abandoned in an alley smack dab in the middle of the Hilltop Gang area. There was of course nothing left inside the car other than the paperwork from the rental car company. After a quick walk around the outside of the car my partner and I both agreed that the car hadn't struck anything during the chase. That was a good thing. We had gotten away with one really great pursuit without it being a "pursuit."

At the end of the day only two things really ended up happening. Me and my partner had gotten a great adrenaline rush, and the rental car company had their car back undamaged. As a caveat to this story: A short time later this same guy shot a man in the parking lot of a Family Dollar store and then got in a legitimate pursuit which ended with Officer's taking shots at him. He was not hit, but he was captured. I'm certain he's still in prison. There is after all only two certainties to the gang lifestyle—death or prison.

WHO KNEW SPIDERS LIKE CRACK

My partner and I were rolling around one spring afternoon when we heard the dispatch of a "suspect wearing a red jersey on the corner selling drugs." The corner in question was the corner of 24th and Pratt Streets; a corner known for drug dealings. It was also in the middle of the area controlled by the Deuce Four Mafia Bloods—that would explain the red jersey. We were only about two blocks away when the call went out so we told dispatch we would handle it.

As we approached the corner we only saw one guy in a red jersey, and it happened to be a gangbanger we dealt with all the time. We parked and got out and as soon as we did the two older crack-heads that were standing there took off. Now we were alone with our guy. I flat out told him somebody called 911 to report a guy in a red jersey selling drugs on the street corner. He of course didn't believe me. No matter, I began to pat-frisk him anyway. I could tell from experience that he had a wad of cash stuffed into his front pockets, along with a cell phone. Like any decent drug dealer he didn't have the drugs on him. I didn't expect to find the drugs on him, which meant he had a stash somewhere nearby and readily accessible. This was my favorite kind of hide-and-seek!

I had my partner watch our guy as I began my hunt for the drugs. The place where we were standing was the back side of a little corner store with apartments above it. There were a few derelict vehicles in the lot, but not much else. I looked for a solid five minutes and didn't find anything. I looked over and our guy was starting to look smug. I took a step back and surveyed the surroundings. I had missed something, I was sure of it. He had the money in his pockets, so the only other possibility was that he was sold out. Not ready to give up yet I took another look next to the building. As I was ducking underneath a fire escape I looked up and there it was; the stash.

I had to give him credit for style and originality. He had hidden his pre-packaged rocks of crack in an old spider web of all things! There they were hanging suspended like flies in the spider web. There were only a couple of rocks left but it was enough for me. Since we didn't actually find the drugs on him we had to go through a few more steps of investigation. We didn't arrest him at that time, but we did take him into custody for transport down to Central Headquarters. Alright, technically that could be considered an arrest since he wasn't free to leave. Anyway, once we made it downtown I had the crime lab technician swab our suspect's hands for drug residue. Those hand swabs would then be sent to the lab to identify any drugs present on the skin of his hands.

I told our suspect the deal: If the hand swabs came back negative for crack-cocaine then I would admit my wrong and apologize. On the other hand, if they came back positive then I would write a Felony Arrest Warrant and come looking for him personally. That was that, we let him walk out the front door of Central. I knew it would take several days for the hand swabs to make it to the lab and back, so I wasn't in a hurry. About four days later I had a copy of the lab report waiting for me in my mailbox at work. The result was not a surprise—positive for cocaine. I wrote the Warrant and found a judge to sign it later that day. The very next day my partner and I found him and arrested him...on the exact same street corner.

2CX BODY REPAIR

I've got to explain the title to this story. "2CX" is a police code describing a person. It has several components so here's the breakdown: The 2 indicates the person has previously been charged with a felony. The C means they were convicted of a felony. The X means the person has a history of violence or a history of using or possessing weapons. As you might assume, a majority of gangbangers are labeled as "2CX." This story involves just such a person.

My first six months in the Gang Unit was not spent on the street. I spent my first six months working in a daytime position as the North Gang Intelligence Officer. It was my job to collect intelligence, write safety bulletins, give public speeches, and pass information to all the cops on the street regarding gang activity. It was a pretty easy gig, but I found it boring. Whenever possible I found excuses to take a car and hit the streets. My Sergeant was pretty hands-off so she indulged my need for street time.

One afternoon I was out killing time when I noticed a brand new maroon Mitsubishi Galant riddled with fresh bullet holes along the driver's side. I called the plate in to dispatch and they advised me it was owned by a rental company. I was not surprised. Most of the hardcore gangbangers conducted their business with rental cars. It was towards the end of my day so I decided to follow up with the rental car company the next day.

    I called the rental company the first thing in the morning when I got to work and asked them to provide me the name of the renter of the shot-up Galant. They told me the car was no longer rented, having been turned in first thing that morning. I had them tell me where the car was turned in so that I could go visit the location manager. They obliged me, and I was on my way.

    I got to the branch location and asked to see the maroon Galant. To my utter amazement there were no holes in the car! I double-checked the license plate on the car. I had the right car. I now had myself a mystery to solve. I told the manager what I had witnessed the previous day. The manager looked at me like I was joking. I assured him I was not. I opened the driver's door and gave it a good shake. There was definitely something rattling inside the car door. I took a look inside and under the front seat I found an empty magazine to a Glock handgun. I could see by the manager's expression he was starting to believe me.

He had his mechanic come over and pop the inside door panel off the driver's door. There was my proof down inside the door; several slugs. Judging by the size of the lead I guessed .45 caliber. Upon closer inspection of the outside of the driver's door we found evidence that bodywork had been done. Having proved my claim the manager provided me with all the information I asked for.

I went to the residence of the lady that had rented the car. She was about twenty-five and looked like she was no stranger to hard life. I noticed she had a tattoo on her arm that said "Flatland." She obviously had allegiance to the Flatland Bloods. She didn't tell me much, but she did tell me that her brother had driven the car. I tracked down her brother, taking one of the slugs from the car door with me for the conversation. He was young, but extremely hard for his age. He just smiled at me and wouldn't tell me anything. I didn't waste my time beating a dead horse. I knew that I would be dealing with this kid again.

THROWING AWAY THE CAR KEYS

The previous story introduced me to a kid that I would have issues with during my entire tenure in the Gang Unit. This story tells how my involvement with the kid ended. I had moved from the Gang Intelligence Unit to the North Gang Suppression Squad. I had my partner, the same one for several years. He and I were quite the team. Many guns we took off the streets of Omaha. This story is about a gun. As I foreshadowed at the end of the last story, I had found a nemesis. It had all started with a rental car full of bullet holes. Over the years it turned into a hate-hate relationship.

My nemesis had established himself as a leader of the Flatland Bloods. I suppose he had no choice. His entire family including his mother and grandmother were all aware of the gang's activities. In the Flatland area is a park called Kountze Park. On any given day when the weather was nice you could find up to a dozen Flatlanders hanging out in the park. Well, it was a nice day so my partner and I were driving through Kountze Park. There he was; my nemesis.

He had been standing next to a parked car until he saw us coming. Like the rest of the gangbangers he could spot our black Dodge Intrepid coming even though it was unmarked. As we came closer he started moving away from the parked car. As he moved away he walked by a park trash can and very smoothly deposited something inside. My partner saw it as well. There had actually been an entire group standing around the car, which again was a rental. Not knowing what we were walking into we immediately had everyone sit on the curb with their backs to the trash can. I walked over to the trash can and looked inside expecting to find a gun or drugs. That's not what I found. I found a set of car keys; the keys to the parked car.

My partner had noticed that the car was parked partially in a handicapped stall which gave us full authority to conduct our investigation. My partner looked into the car via the open driver's side window and there on the floor was a chrome plated .45 caliber 1911. Now it made sense why our suspect had thrown away the car keys—those keys tied him to the car, and the car tied him to the gun. I stood him up and cuffed him. I had waited a long time to catch him with a gun. As it turned out it was a stolen gun.

Because of his gang ties and his criminal history we were able to Federally Indict my nemesis. It wasn't easy. He put up a very good defense. We had to make it past an evidence suppression hearing, which we won. When it was all said and done he went to Federal prison. In the meantime I retired. What a great way to end our relationship.

C.C.W. TRIFECTA

Many times in my career I ran into people and I had to ask myself: Just what makes them tick? This is a story of one of those people. It started off as a traffic stop for a broken tail light. There were two people in the car; driver and front seat passenger. I was riding with another Officer that night and he was driving so he made approach on the driver's side, while I approached on the passenger side of the car. Right away I could tell the passenger was nervous. I couldn't see any danger cues inside the car, but my gut instinct was telling me something was amiss.

I asked the passenger if there were any weapons in the car. He hesitated with a long pause before answering "No." I didn't believe him. I had my partner meet me at the back of the car and told him my suspicions. My partner and I decided it would be prudent to ask the driver the same question. If he responded no, then we would ask for permission to search the vehicle. When asked, the driver advised us that "He wasn't aware of any weapons in his vehicle." Good we said. There shouldn't be any problem with us taking a quick look just to be sure. The driver agreed and gave us verbal consent to search the car.

We had both occupants step out of the car. My partner patted down the driver and didn't find anything. I patted down the passenger and found what I had suspected. In his back pocket he had a pair of brass knuckles which are considered by law to be a concealed weapon. I placed him under arrest and resumed my search of his pockets. In his front right pocket I found a huge folding knife, also a concealed weapon. After depriving him of all his weapons I secured him in the cruiser. We hadn't even made it to the vehicle search yet!

My partner searched the driver's side and didn't find anything of note. I on the other hand did. Concealed under the front passenger seat was a loaded .38 snub nose revolver. I now fully understood why the passenger had been so nervous. I went back to the cruiser and verbally mirandized the passenger. I asked him what possible reason he had for carrying three different types of illegal concealed weapons. His only response was "People were trying to get him." I left it at that since the case was pretty clear cut and I didn't need any admissions to prove him guilty.

By policy any time you caught somebody with a concealed weapon, much less three of them, it was mandatory to book the person into jail. We kicked the driver loose with his traffic ticket and then headed for Central with our arrestee. All of his charges were misdemeanor so he could bond out providing he had the money.

I went to court on the day of the trial wondering what the judge was going to hand down as a sentence. One day in jail, time served. Oh well, another illegal firearm off the streets.

PROFESSIONAL INSTALL

Good drug dealers are hard to catch. Here's an example. I had just gotten a partner upon transferring to the northeast precinct. He was showing me around the precinct and we stopped in an apartment complex called Tommie Rose Gardens. They are since long gone. The apartments were run by the Hilltop Crips; lots of drug dealing going on. We pulled into one of the apartment parking lots and my partner instantly set his sights on a carload full of guys. There were four guys sitting in a nice Chevrolet Caprice smoking weed.

We got them out and took away all their individual bags of weed. They were all small bags, not even a misdemeanor crime. I did a search of the car and didn't find anything else. My partner then asked me to watch the suspects while he did a search of the car. I was kind of insulted; didn't he think I was capable of searching a car for drugs? As he began his search another cruiser pulled up and I had the Officers in that car watch our suspects. I wanted to see what my partner was going to do that I already hadn't.

I could tell that my partner was intently studying the dashboard of the car. It had a really nice aftermarket stereo system that looked like a complete custom install. After a few minutes my partner got out his folding knife and asked me if I saw anything suspicious on the dashboard. I told him I saw a really expensive looking stereo. He then showed me a blank faceplate just beneath the stereo where an ashtray would normally be in that year of Chevy Caprice. He specifically pointed out some small scratches on the top edge of that faceplate. I could see the scratches but was failing to make the connection. My partner then gently inserted the tip of his knife into the seam above the faceplate and pried outward. The entire faceplate popped completely out and there hiding in a concealed compartment was a golf ball sized bag of crack-cocaine. For those of you that aren't a drug dealer or a cop, I will tell you that is a substantial amount of crack.

I was so impressed by my partner's savvy find that I took several nice Polaroids of the compartment both closed and open and forwarded them to the training academy. Within a week a training bulletin featuring those pictures was published for everyone's benefit. I for one had learned a valuable hands-on lesson.

I FELL ON THE GUN

It was my first year on the Gang Unit and we were patrolling Tommie Rose Garden apartments looking for Hilltop Crips doing dirt. It was near to impossible to sneak up on the gangbangers due to the layout of the buildings. I suppose that's why they liked to hang out there so much. We had a strategy to combat the lack of stealth. It was completely simple—haul ass as fast as possible into the parking lot and jump out of the cruiser. After all, that is how we earned the nickname "The jump-out boys." The strategy worked great due to the simplicity. Catch the bad guys off guard and the guilty ones would run almost without fail. It was almost like science.

That was what we did on this night. Immediately a guy standing next to the corner of one of the buildings took off running down a hill westbound. They run, we chase; that was our mantra. My partner and I both took off after the suspect, my partner slightly ahead of me. As we ran down the hill we encountered a flight of stairs along the slope. The suspect and my partner both jumped the entire flight of stairs and landed without falling. To this day I don't know how they made the jump without collapsing with broken legs. I chose the path of least resistance and ran around the stairs.

After about two hundred yards we had left the apartments behind and were coming up on an abandoned building. My partner and I each took a side of the building and ended up catching the guy on the far side. My partner cuffed the suspect and started the long walk back up the hill to our cruiser. I began the hunt for whatever caused him to run in the first place. I had almost made it back to the cruiser when I found it; a .357 magnum revolver. The suspect must have dropped it shortly after he took off running.

We transported him down to Central and I conducted an interview which I recorded with audio and video. In my interview I used the simplest and easiest bluff in the world. I told him we had the crime lab test the gun for fingerprints and had his prints on the gun. I asked him straight out, "How do you explain that your fingerprints are on the gun we found?" He looked at me with a straight face and said "I must have fallen on the gun while you were chasing me!" He even did a re-enactment for my benefit. Close enough to a confession for me. The Feds agreed and indicted him.

ONE GUN GOOD, TWO GUNS BETTER

My partner and I were patrolling yet another gathering spot for the Hilltop Crips, a place called the Spencer Projects. It was winter so everyone was wearing big puffy coats which made it harder to pick out the gangbangers. We had just pulled into the apartments when a guy walking towards us did a military style about face. It was so blatantly obvious it was comical. My partner almost threw me out of the cruiser and said "Go get that guy!" So I jumped out and hollered to the guy to come and talk to me. Instead he took off running. I had expected it so I had actually started running the minute I exited the cruiser. I caught up to him just as he reached an apartment door. As he fumbled with the handle I pancake blocked him in the back, knocking the wind out of him.

He was pretty stunned so I didn't have any trouble getting the cuffs on him, except for the big puffy coat getting in my way. Since I had him pressed against the door I decided to start searching his rear pockets first. The first thing I found was a loaded .25 caliber magazine. My partner had caught up to us so I handed him the magazine. I searched his waistband and front pockets but didn't find the gun I was looking for. Finally I searched his coat pockets. In his left coat pocket I found a .25 caliber Jennings handgun. Jennings made about the cheapest firearm available so we encountered them all the time. The last place I checked was his right coat pocket. I couldn't believe it. I found another .25 Jennings identical to the other one. So this guy had matching handguns and an extra loaded magazine in his pocket!

We put the guy in our cruiser and started talking to him. He turned out to be a pretty nice guy. He explained that some guys were after him over something to do with his family. This guy we had wasn't even in a gang. Policy is policy so we had to book the guy into jail. I couldn't help feeling bad for him, so I think the last thing I said to him was "I'm sorry."

C.C.W. SELFIE

One of the mandatory tasks we did have on the Gang Unit was working big events at the high schools like dances. It wasn't too bad and we usually ended up finding something good by the end of the night. We didn't have to actually go inside and chaperone, we more or less just loitered in the parking lot and deterred gang violence.

We were working a dance at North High School and were bored because nothing was going on. I happened to note however, that several guys across the street were loitering in the yard of an abandoned house that was posted no trespassing. This was one of my favorite scenarios. Gangbangers and drug dealers love to use abandoned houses for the crimes. It made it easy when you knew the person in the front yard didn't live there. It was as simple as walking up and saying "What the hell are you doing here?"

We got out of our cruiser and left it in the parking lot of the high school while we walked across the street. One guy did a quick fade around the corner of the house and I figured he was gone, but then he reappeared. That sort of act was always a good indicator. We made it across the street and nobody took off running. I had my partner engage the fellas in conversation while I went around the side of the house. It took me a couple of minutes but I found a chrome plated .40 caliber stashed under a drain pipe. I rejoined my partner in front with the group and promptly cuffed the guy that had "faded" prior to our arrival. I told him he was technically under arrest for trespassing. As I searched him I found his cell phone in his pocket. Then I found part of a cell phone in his left sock, and the battery and back to the phone in his right sock. I put the parts back together and powered up cell phone number two. I began looking through his pictures and found exactly what I had hoped to find.

Gangbangers for whatever reason love to take pictures of themselves with their guns, drugs, and money. In this case our suspect had taken several nice self-shot pictures in a mirror holding a gun that looked exactly like the gun currently lying around the corner of the house. Furthermore, he had sent several texts describing his .40 caliber to his buddies. I forgot to mention that we had previously caught the same kid before with a gun so this second offense was enhanced to a felony. He tried to get the cell phone information suppressed as inadmissible, but he failed. He was convicted and I had made another life-long enemy.

NICE SHOOTING, YOU GOT'EM BOTH

I told a story earlier about pepperball guns; fun to use on others, not fun when used on you. Being a high speed rookie when the department decided to get pepperball guns, I immediately signed up for the certification class. For the most part it was classroom instruction on the legalities of using them—when you could, couldn't, should, and shouldn't. I understand that stuff is important to know, but I wanted to shoot the things! Unfortunately we weren't allowed to touch the pepperball guns until we had been shot with one.

The whole rationale behind getting shot is for possible future court testimony. Just like with the departmental issued pepper spray (which we also got shot with in the academy) you had to be able to defend your usage on the stand if asked. I didn't like the prospect of getting shot, especially after seeing the video produced by the manufacturer. I supposed it was only temporary pain and I considered myself to be on the tougher end of the spectrum.

I think the worst part was the anticipation. The instructors were all on the S.W.A.T. team so they thought it was a good idea for all of us to stand in a line and watch the shooting until it was our turn. One by one I watched my fellow Officers get shot by two rounds from the pepperball gun. I was toward the back of the line, and after watching the first ten or so get shot I was beginning to have second thoughts. At long last it was my turn. It was summer so all I was wearing was a thin t-shirt. I looked at the instructor holding the pepperball gun, who by the way was having too much fun. I knew him pretty well, and he knew I was pretty cocky. I'm pretty sure these facts dictated what happened next.

    I stood there about twenty feet in front of the instructor with my hands covering my groin in the event of an errant shot. The odds of an errant shot were slim to none; this was after all a S.W.A.T. team member. I braced myself and he asked me if I was ready. I nodded yes. I heard the sound of the double tap and instantly felt the most intense stinging sensation I had ever felt! I knew the instructor was a good shot, but I didn't realize just how good. He had managed to hit me squarely in BOTH nipples. Not just one, but both! I dropped to my knees in agony to the sounds of my co-workers laughing hysterically. Everybody before me had taken shots to the thighs or shoulders. I had obviously been singled out. I recovered enough to make it to the bathroom and pull my shirt up. Both my nipples were already black and blue and purple and swollen. I had definitely earned the right to carry a pepperball gun.

LESS IS MORE

As I've said before, I learned more watching the veteran cops than I ever did sitting in a chair in the academy. There were certain cops that you just knew were born to be cops. I mentioned a cop in a previous story; the one that could tell a crack dealer with a simple wave from a street corner. I made it a point to watch him for my entire career since he was such a living legend. One thing I always noticed about him was his seeming disregard for some of the pages out of the department's Standard Operating Procedures manual. I must admit, I tended to agree with him on a lot of the finer points. Some things work great on paper, and not so well on the streets.

One thing I noticed about this particular cop was how year after year his duty gun-belt seemed to be more and more Spartan. Pretty soon I found myself doing the same thing. Some items were mandated to be on your gun-belt, and twice a year your gear had to pass official inspection. The real issue for me was carrying all the extra weight; it really tended to slow you down. For somebody like me, any pound that I could shave meant I was one step quicker in the foot chases. Many times in the foot chases that one step meant the difference between catching your suspect and watching your suspect get away.

Year after year I found my gun-belt lacking many of the required items. For example: I quit carrying pepper spray and a baton. I never carried a taser. I found over the years that less is more. I used to love watching the rookies coming out of the academy. There wasn't an unused spot on many of their gun-belts. On a lot of them you couldn't even see the leather belt! They had added second flashlights, Gerber multi-tools, extra handcuffs, glove pouches; the list goes on. I also noticed that a lot of those same rookies were terribly slow getting out of the cruiser because all their gear caught on everything and drastically cut down on their mobility.

By my last year I had learned from the legend. My duty gun-belt was down to my gun, two extra magazines, a flashlight, and handcuffs. Ninety-nine percent of the time that was all I ever needed. For the remaining one percent of the time there was always a rookie close by when you needed something else.

ROLL YOUR WINDOWS UP WHEN IGNORING DIRECTIONS

The entire northeast precinct was on full alert every other year for an event called "Native Omaha Days." Every other year people from all over the country that were originally from Omaha would come back for the weekend festival. The vast majority of the people were there to have a good time. The problem was the gangbangers. They found it the perfect opportunity to basically practice civil unrest. As a result, every cop ended up working a ton of overtime. For the Gang Unit it was non-stop for about seventy-two hours.

I remember one year in particular the crowds were especially large, and the gangbangers were particularly out of control. At one point a lot of cops including yours truly got stuck doing traffic control at key intersections. There were about six of us stuck working the intersection of 30th and Ames Avenue. This was always a problem intersection even when there wasn't a special event going on. We had traffic routed only north and south; east and west were closed so that we could maintain some semblance of control. That was our plan. It never failed. One person always had to buck the plan.

One of the cops working the corner had a pepperball gun hanging over his shoulder by a sling. This cop also happened to be the son of a Deputy Chief. He was as by-the-book as they come. This was understandable given who his father was.

As we stood there directing traffic we encountered the one person who wanted to defy the system. The driver of a Jeep Cherokee had it in his head that he was going to turn eastbound and didn't care what we were screaming at him. Native Omaha Days always happened during the summer so this driver had every window in his Jeep rolled down. He literally drove around two of us to try and make his eastbound turn. I was just about to kick the side of his Jeep out of pure anger and frustration when all of the sudden I heard the tell-tale sound of a pepperball gun being fired in rapid succession. The driver was about halfway through his turn when a barrage of about twenty pepperballs travelled through his passenger side window. I know for a fact that several of the projectiles connected squarely on the side of his head! I thought to myself "Holy crap. That had to hurt!" Not to mention the instant cloud of pepper powder that had enveloped the interior of the Jeep. The driver was able to finish the turn...just barely. He bounced off the curb and then took out a trash can before regaining control of the vehicle. We all turned dumbfounded to the cop that had fired the rounds. He was smiling from ear to ear. Pretty soon we all were. What we had just witnessed was so out of character for the Deputy Chief's son. Not one word was ever spoken about the incident after that night. It was just better that way.

DIRECT LINE

This story takes place towards the end of my time in the Gang Unit. My partner and I were just starting a shift. We were into our usual routine, just patrolling the gang hot spots looking for trouble. We got behind a car that had two guys we recognized as Murdertown Crips. They pulled a common trick. As soon as we got behind them they pulled into the first available driveway, parked, got out, and went to the front door and pretended to knock. We had seen this trick before and weren't falling for it. We called their bluff and pulled into the driveway right behind them. I walked right past the two guys and really knocked on the front door. A kindly little old woman answered the door and I asked her if she knew either of the two guys standing on her front porch. She answered no, and added that she would like them removed from her property.

As we were conducting our business a well known violent gangbanger had been mowing the yard of the house next door to where we were. When I say violent I mean this; he once shot several holes in an unmarked police car while two Gang Unit Detectives were inside. We had the two guys down in the driveway at this point and were running them for warrants. In the middle of this, the thug from next door walked over with his cell phone and said "Yall's boss wants to talk to you." He shoved the cell phone in my face as he said it. I was livid. I told him to "Get the hell out of my face and go back to the other yard!"

It turned out one of the guys we were checking had outstanding arrest warrants. We cuffed him and put him in the cruiser, and kicked the other guy out of the area. We had just pulled out of the driveway en-route for Central when my departmental issue phone rang. It was our Sergeant and he wanted to know what we were doing. I told him what we had just finished doing and then asked him why he wanted to know. I didn't get a straight answer. With that said, I was left to wonder how in the world a gangbanger could have such an easy time getting into my business. The only logical conclusion I could reach was that he had the ear of somebody WAY up the command chain. It was totally disheartening to think that a violent gangbanger could reach out to upper command easier than I could at the drop of a hat. I kick myself for not taking that cell phone when he shoved it in my face. It would be nice to know who was on the other end of that phone. I have my suspicions. If you ever see me in person ask and I'll tell you who I think it was.

IF I'M THE FIFTH, THERE WON'T BE A SIXTH

There was a kid I dealt with constantly while on the Gang Unit nicknamed "Knuckles." He was a Hilltop Crip, but he never really did much. I think he was in the gang by default; all of his friends were in the gang so he was too. He was actually pretty sociable and always had a smile on his face. He got the nickname Knuckles because the first time he was shot it was in the hand. He had a bad habit of always being visible, especially to rival gang members. I remember one summer he got shot at twice in a month at the same gas station. I remember asking him once why he didn't take a lower profile. He just smiled at me.

One of his favorite spots to hang out with his buddies was a group of city run apartments called the Pleasantview Projects. They were there all the time. Because they were always there, my partner and I made it a point to spend a lot of time there as well. Many times we would park off on a side street and walk into the courtyard areas just to catch them off guard. Many times it would result in a foot chase, which was always fun.

We were doing a walk through one summer night and ran into a group of about six gang members. One of the rules of the city run apartments was that you were subject to police contact at the discretion of the police. Even when nobody ran from us we made it a point to always check everyone for outstanding arrest warrants. We were in the process of doing just that when completely out of the blue Knuckles asked me "If I pulled out a cell phone really fast and pointed it at you would you shoot me?" I pondered his question and asked him in return, "Knuckles, how many times have you actually been shot, not just shot at?" He answered four times. I told him "Knuckles, if I'm the fifth person to shoot you, then there won't be a sixth." His buddies all started laughing. Knuckles just gave me the usual smile.

CRUISER STRIP SEARCH BLUFF

Over the years I found that some of the best police work was not done with your hands, but rather with your mind. The only fight you could truly ever win was the one you didn't fight. I made it through my entire career without ever missing a day due to injury. I attribute that to the fact that I tried to be a thinker, not a fighter. Strategy and tactics go a long way to keeping you out of dangerous situations. They could also be the foundation of great investigations.

My partner and I put this philosophy into practice with one of our daily routines. Every day before leaving the precinct parking lot we would thoroughly check the back seat of the cruiser for any contraband wedged down into the seam of the seat. We did this to ensure that nothing was there prior to putting any suspects in our back seat. It seems like something very simple, but it also turned out to be a very effective way to catch a drug dealer.

Drug dealers love to hide drugs in the crack of their ass, or in their underwear. This is common knowledge. It is also common knowledge that a person in handcuffs can always manage to remove their drugs given the proper motivation. This is where the strategy and tactics come into play.

Whenever my partner and I ran across someone that we thought was holding drugs we employed our simple ruse. It went like this: First you have to put the person in the back of the cruiser. Sometimes that was in handcuffs, sometimes it wasn't. The rear windows had to be down so that the person in the backseat could hear you. Then you had to make them nervous, really nervous about what was going to happen to them. The way we did that was to stand at the front of the cruiser and engage in conversation. Inevitably that conversation would by design turn to the topic of a strip search. Most of the time we had nowhere near enough probable cause or suspicion to warrant a strip search, but that was irrelevant. The whole goal of the ruse was to make sure the person in the back seat heard our conversation and believed we had every intention of conducting a strip search. Fear of being caught is a powerful motivator. After a time we would then remove the person from the back seat and take them a short distance from the cruiser while one of us kept them engaged in conversation. It was important to make sure the person had their back to the cruiser since whoever wasn't talking was conducting a search of the back seat.

I can't tell you how many times we would find baggies of assorted drugs stuffed into the crease of the back seat. Knowing that there weren't any drugs there previously was all the probable cause needed to make the arrest for the recovered drugs. I never had one case dismissed as the result of that strategy. There's nothing more satisfying than getting suspects to basically tell on themselves.

NICE DOG BARK

Lots of times during foot chases the suspect would get away; temporarily. It was rare that a suspect had the speed and opportunity to completely disappear during a foot chase. The majority of the time if the suspect did get away it meant they had a friendly house close by where they could hide until the cops gave up and left. For the rest of the times when you could no longer see them it meant they were hiding somewhere nearby. If it was nighttime and the helicopter was flying then the Forward Looking Infrared camera system was great for finding a hiding suspect.

Lots of my foot chases happened during the daylight hours. It's much harder to hide during the daytime. The best way to find a hidden suspect during the day is with a good **K-9**. They are also a great tool when it's dark. Once you know you have a suspect trapped in a perimeter it becomes a slow moving game. The longest part of the game is getting the **K-9** dog to your scene. Once the **K-9** arrives it goes back to the principles of strategy and tactics.

In all the **K-9** apprehensions I witnessed over the years very few suspects actually got bitten. Suspects hate service dogs. The threat of getting bitten is usually enough to flush a suspect from a hiding spot. The best way to let them know the dog is there is to get the dog barking. Not just barking, but snarling and making all the noises that an amped up K-9 makes when they think they're going to get to find someone. A good handler can get their dog barking on command. It's really fun to watch.

This story is about a foot chase and the sound of a dog barking; except it wasn't really a dog at all. We had chased a gangbanger into a residential neighborhood and lost sight of him. He was one of the well known guys. We were pretty certain the suspect was pinned down somewhere close by so we called the dispatcher and asked for a K-9. As it turned out none were available due to joint training being conducted with some of the other local agencies. We were about to give up when I remembered that the guy we were chasing might have been bitten once before by a K-9. Maybe all wasn't lost!

We had a cop that worked northeast that had an amazing ability to imitate sounds. His best two imitations were a fire truck siren, and a dog bark. He happened to be there on the perimeter so I went over and found him. I told him my plan and he thought he could pull it off. He pulled his cruiser into an alley where we had our last visual sight of the fleeing suspect. He fired up the P.A. system and did his best imitation of a police K-9. It was amazing how real it sounded. Well it must have sounded real enough to our hidden suspect because he came walking out of a shed by the alley and surrendered. The ironic part was we had already checked that shed and determined there was too much crap in it for someone to hide. That in and of itself is a valuable lesson—people can hide in places you wouldn't believe possible.

AIRPORT DUI

During my career I didn't arrest too many people for Driving Under the Influence. It took too much time, required too much paperwork, and generally annoyed me to have to deal with the drunks. Lots of Officers loved to arrest for DUI's because it was guaranteed court time which translated into overtime and money. There were the occasional times however when I had no choice. This is my favorite DUI story.

My partner and I were called to the Eppley Airport for a DUI. Already this call was strange. I had never heard of someone driving drunk in an airport, at least not getting caught doing it! At least this would be interesting. We got to the airport and were met by an Airport Police Officer. The airport does maintain its own department, but for whatever reason they wanted us to handle this particular problem. We had expected to see a car pulled over somewhere but we didn't. The airport cop then took us on a walk to the side of the airport terminal building. There was a car parked directly next to the terminal, and inside there was a guy.

From there it got comical really quickly. As we looked into the parked car the first thing we saw was the driver, completely passed out in the driver's seat with the car still running. The second thing we saw was an empty 750ml bottle of vodka on the passenger seat. The final thing that caught our eye was the "NO PARKING" sign in the back seat. Apparently our guy wanted the V.I.P. parking so he had actually ripped the NO PARKING sign off the side of the terminal building. It was plainly obvious from the non-faded bricks where the sign was supposed to be hanging.

We decided the last thing we needed was this character waking up and trying to drive out of the airport, or over us. Luckily the driver's door was unlocked so I reached in and turned the car off and kept the keys. Our next step was to wake this guy up. This proved to be the hardest part of the entire process. At long last we got him awake. He was completely disoriented and didn't even believe, or know why he was at the airport. He was so drunk it was impossible to conduct even the most simple of the field sobriety tests. We were able to get him to blow into the breathalyzer, which yielded a result over .30. Thankfully he was a happy drunk and not a mean drunk. He was totally cooperative and just wanted to get to Central Headquarters so he could go back to sleep.

WALKING THE DEUCE STRAPPED

If something doesn't look right, then it probably isn't. This is one of my rules to live by. My partner and I were walking the "Deuce." This is the slang term for 24th Street in north Omaha. We were out on foot patrol sneaking around looking for Deuce Four Mafia Bloods. The residents of the area are predominantly Black. As we were walking we noticed a lone Hispanic kid about fourteen or fifteen walking through the yard of a community resource building. We worked that area all the time and had never seen any Hispanic kids that we could remember. Being smack dab in the middle of Deuce Four land I was kind of concerned for this kid in the event some of the local gangbangers decided to mess with him.

I walked up to him to ask what he was doing and if he knew where he was. As I got to within about six feet from this kid I could see the outline of a gun handle through his shirt. I immediately drew down on him and backed up a few feet. This kid was completely calm and seemed to be totally comfortable with me pointing my gun at his head. My partner was quite a ways off and didn't see what was happening. I was on my own. I instantly thought to myself it sure would be nice to have a witness if I had to shoot this kid!

I slowly and deliberately gave him verbal commands to pull up his shirt. I wanted to see that it truly was a gun under his shirt and I wasn't just imagining things. He complied and lifted up his shirt. I was right; it was a brown handled revolver in his waistband. My partner had finally taken note and was now sprinting to my location. I had the kid put his hands on his head. I wanted his hands as far away as possible from that gun until my partner got there.

It didn't take long before my partner had the kid in cuffs and we had the gun in our possession. We took him back to the precinct building to attempt an interview and do some research on the gun. The kid didn't want to talk. The gun had been defaced in several ways. It was a .357 magnum with the barrel partially sawed off. Additionally, the serial number had been filed off, making it impossible to see if it was stolen. Possession of a defaced firearm is an automatic felony charge.

We took the kid to the Juvenile Detention Facility and dropped him off. I assumed that was the end of the case. A couple of weeks later I got a call from the Deputy County Attorney handling the case. She wanted to know if the kid knew the firearm was defaced. I told her I didn't know, nor did I care since the statute didn't state anything about the suspect's knowledge regarding the defacement. She had a dissenting opinion, and after all she was the County Attorney. Ultimately the kid's charge got reduced from a felony to a misdemeanor "Carrying a Concealed Weapon." The reduction in charge will play out in the next story.

THE DEUCE CONTINUED

On November 12th, 2008 three gang members went on a robbery and shooting spree that eventually left two people dead and a third injured. The city of Omaha was horrified by the acts. They were seemingly random and utterly senseless crimes. I didn't actually work any part of the case since the gang members were from south of Dodge Street, and I worked the gangs north of Dodge. I remember reading the internal e-mail "Overnight Report" regarding the incident the next day. I always made it a practice to read every noteworthy event that occurred in the city because I felt it made me a better cop.

As I read the gruesome account of what the three gangbangers had done I felt the usual anger at such senseless killing. Then I got to the end of the e-mail and read the names of the three suspects. My heart immediately sank. One of the suspects was the kid my partner and I had arrested just a couple months prior with the defaced firearm on 24th Street. Apparently he wasn't locked up like he should have been. Then I remembered. The felony we arrested him on got knocked down to a misdemeanor. That would explain why he was out on the streets to commit more crimes.

I don't know if anything would have turned out different if the felony charge had stuck and the kid had been locked up for a longer sentence. Maybe it would have turned out exactly the same. I don't know. I just hate having to ponder the question "What if?"

DON'T THROW COCKED REVOLVERS

Driving around in unmarked Gang Unit cruisers had an inherent element of risk. This story will make that clear. We were riding three deep in the car on this particular night because we were doing an orientation of sorts with an Officer new to the Gang Unit. We were showing her the "hot-spots" in the hopes of running into some of the regulars. It was dark out and we were cruising in the area controlled by the 40th Avenue Crips. This was one of my personal favorite areas because it was usually active and there were a lot of guns floating around.

We had started to make our way to the fringe of the area and were on 43rd Avenue when we saw three guys walking down the middle of the street. Omaha had a city ordinance which prohibited walking in the street if a sidewalk was available. It was technically an arrest grade offense so we used it all the time. Not because we cared about people walking in the street, because it gave us a reason to get out and pat people down for weapons.

We pulled up quick behind them and did our "jump-out." Believe it or not the three gave a sigh and had relieved looks on their faces. We actually experienced this reaction fairly often. The gangbangers were actually glad sometimes when it was the police and not a rival gang getting ready to blast on them. This is the effect of riding around in unmarked cruisers. We started in with our usual routine, explaining that it was illegal to walk down the middle of the street so a pat-down was coming. Nobody ran so I assumed we were "88" meaning no problems at hand. There is an old adage about making assumptions. I started to pat down the guy closest to me and immediately felt a gun in his right coat pocket. I announced out loud "gun" so that my two partners could react appropriately with their respective suspects. Then I did something really stupid.

I made the split second decision to reach into the suspect's pocket and grab the gun which turned out to be a .38 revolver. I then threw the gun and sent it skidding across the pavement. I figured it was better to have the gun out of the equation when I went to handcuff my suspect. I handcuffed him and sat him down while my partners searched their suspects. Nothing else was found so we kicked the other two guys loose.

I meanwhile went over to retrieve the gun that I had thrown. As I picked it up I had one of those "Oh shit" moments. The hammer on the revolver was pulled back. I was extremely lucky the gun had landed in such a manner so as not to knock the hammer forward. If that hammer would have slammed forward it would have fired a round.

We got our suspect in the car and I asked him why he had the hammer cocked. He answered "We didn't know you were cops, we thought we were about to get shot at." That seemed reasonable to me.

PREP THE ROOM FOR THE FIGHT

We were on the way to a domestic disturbance call. We got there and found that the husband had beaten up his wife. Per state law we had to arrest the husband. He knew that and didn't seem to care all that much. It's important to mention the husband weighed 400 pounds, at least. He was sitting calmly in a chair throughout our initial investigation with the wife. The dispatcher apparently knew about the size of the suspect so three Officers had been dispatched instead of the normal two. After seeing the guy and his demeanor I called for our Sergeant to come to the scene. Before long there were three Officers and a Sergeant staring at the huge man in the chair. It was an uncomfortably long silent period before the suspect spoke up and indicated he wasn't going to go easily.

Our Sergeant, worried about the level of force that might be required called for the Precinct Lieutenant to come to the scene. Our Lieutenant was a huge man in his own right. So there we all sat just staring at each other while we waited for the Lieutenant to arrive. It was surreal. Most domestic disturbance calls were highly dynamic and fast paced. This one was the exact opposite.

Our Lieutenant finally arrived and made one last attempt at gaining this guy's cooperation. It was to no avail. The Lieutenant shrugged his shoulders and started moving furniture. The most prominent piece of furniture in the room was a huge glass coffee table. The table was the first thing to get moved to a corner. I couldn't believe we were actually prepping the room for the fight. It was just so weird how everything was progressing so slowly. Finally, it was time.

I was the first to move in and grab an arm. What an effort in futility; the man was a mountain! It finally took us dumping him out of the chair to really get the fight underway. Once out of the chair it didn't get any easier. We punched, pulled, knee struck, pressure pointed, and used every tactic imaginable. The only reason we were eventually successful was because the guy was just so out of shape. He wasn't the only one that was tired, we were all completely exhausted. He was so inflexible we had to string three pairs of handcuffs together to get him secured. We thought the worst of it was over; were we wrong. The guy made good on his word not to cooperate.

We ended up having to call two more Officers to the scene to get his dead weight lifted into the back seat of a cruiser. It was the same problem getting him into his cell. I went home tired that night.

MY SPECIAL UNDERWEAR

Confidential informants can be a pain in the ass to work with, but they are unfortunately a part of doing business. We had a confidential informant that came to us claiming he could call a guy in Lincoln, and that guy would deliver crack-cocaine to anywhere he wanted. My Sergeant liked the idea so we organized a sting operation. We picked an abandoned house and had our informant make the call to the dealer. The call was successful and the dealer indicated he was leaving Lincoln to make the drive to Omaha. In the meantime our entire Gang Unit crew sat in the back of an unmarked van outside the delivery address waiting to ambush the dealer upon his arrival.

It was a straightforward plan. We would wait for the dealer to pull into the driveway, then pull in behind and block him in. From there it was a matter of jumping out and scaring the dealer and whoever else might be with him into submission. The plan went flawlessly. People tend to cooperate with six cops pointing guns at their heads while screaming directions.

We searched the car and didn't find anything so we let the two females he had brought with him take the car. We transported our suspected dealer to the precinct building for his strip search. We hadn't found the crack in his pockets, so the strip search was inevitable. We got started and didn't find it in his shoes. I wish we would have, it would have spared us the rest of the search. One by one his articles of clothing were taken off until he was down to his underwear. Time for the nasty part. My partner had him remove his underwear and hand them to me. Then, just like in a prison search, bend over and spread your cheeks—nothing! That was not good. We should have found the drugs. I went back through every piece of clothing; it had to be there.

      Finally I was down to the last item. I held in my hands another man's underwear. Thank God for latex gloves. I started feeling his underwear by rolling it between my fingers. Then I found it, the tell-tale lump of crack! The problem was I couldn't figure out how to grab it. It took me a while to figure it out. This guy had gone to the trouble to sew an extra pouch into the bottom of his tighty-whities that was only accessible through the front seam that you pee from. I got it out and found it to be exactly what the confidential informant had ordered: an 8-ball of crack. Mission a success.

EASTER EGG GUN HUNT

Calls had been coming in to the 911 dispatcher of a large crowd gathering at 25th and Maple Street. This was ground-zero for the Deuce Four Mafia Bloods. Our Sergeant got a call from the dispatcher, which meant the entire North Gang Suppression Squad would be headed to 25th and Maple. It was a summer night about 7:00 P.M. so there was plenty of daylight left. As we pulled into the area it was kind of creepy. There were Deuce Four members standing all over the place. They weren't doing anything, just standing around. Nobody took off running so unfortunately there was no one to chase.

Our Sergeant was with us so we had to make a good showing of our work ethic. The largest numbers of gangbangers were standing in the front yard of an abandoned house, so that's where we decided to start snooping. As we made our way into the yard the bangers meandered off to the yard next door. They were all just staring at us. Two of our group posted up to watch the crowd as they watched us. We certainly didn't want to fall victim to any sort of surprise attack, especially since we were so outnumbered.

The abandoned house and yard was a filthy mess. I was on the search team so it was time to find something good for the Sergeant. I found gun number one in the very first place I looked; under an old tire. Before long someone else found a gun wedged in a hollow spot in a tree. A third gun was found in an old BBQ grill. A fourth and fifth gun were found on the porch under old clothes. We had done well. Truth be told we probably missed at least one or two guns. We had all the guns tested for fingerprints by the crime lab, but no usable prints were found. The only thing we could surmise is that we had probably interrupted an impending shootout between the Deuce Four guys and some other rival gang—just another day in the Gang Unit.

HOUSE PARTY GUNS

The call came in as a burglary. Well, that wasn't really what it was. It wasn't the Gang Unit's job to take radio calls but we were close and it sounded fun so we decided to go in with the Uniform Patrol Officers. What the call turned out to be was a house party in an abandoned house. Gangbangers simply love abandoned houses. This particular house was in the middle of the 29th Street Bloods area. We entered the house through a kicked in side door. We had the Uniformed Officers waiting at the front door for everyone to start running out. The minute the party goers saw us coming it started a flood towards the front door. They threw the door open and there were the other cops. This was a full house of people; so full that we really couldn't get all the way in.

One by one people were let out the front door after being patted down for weapons. Word spread quickly that the cops were searching everyone leaving. I told my partner we'd find a bunch of guns by the time it was over. We waited for the last of the people to leave through the front door and then we started snooping. The house was abandoned but there was still furniture inside. It was like shooting fish in a barrel. As we opened up drawers and opened closets we found gun after gun. The best find of the night was by a Uniformed Officer. He found a sealed plastic bag containing three handguns inside the toilet tank in the upstairs bathroom. That's good police work.

JUMPED WITH THE FAMILY

My wife caught wind of an auction she wanted to attend. An Omaha landmark Mr. C's Italian restaurant was closing and they were selling literally everything inside and outside of the building. My wife had her heart set on going so I knew there was no way I was getting out of it. It was a Saturday and I had to work so we had to take separate cars. The plan was to attend the auction, then she would go home and I would go to work. The restaurant was located at 30th and Fort Street, right in the middle of the 29th Street Bloods turf. I was in the Gang Unit at that point so I wasn't thrilled about my wife and baby daughter hanging out in the neighborhood.

We spent a couple hours looking at all the stuff and my wife had bought a hideous outdoor statue. We were just getting ready to leave because it was getting close to the time I had to be to work. We walked out the front door of the restaurant into a patio area and my worst fears came true. Standing directly in my path was three members of the 29th Street Bloods. I was hoping they wouldn't recognize me in street clothes but I was wrong. I pushed my wife and the stroller out of the way and walked towards the three. There was a substantial crowd standing around so I wondered how bold the three would be.

It turned out they wanted to get stupid. They began yelling at me with taunts like "You're not so tough without your partners are ya?" And "Where's your gun and badge?" This was not going the way I wanted. By now people were starting to take note of the conflict. The three started towards me and they forced my hand. I pulled my shirt up to show them that I had a gun on my belt. Seeing a gun panicked the crowd so I had to calm all of them down. Luckily I had my badge to support my story. In the confusion the three bangers had fled out the front gate.

I got my wife and daughter out of there safely and went to work. It was plainly clear that I had some people to track down later that night. I told my crew what had happened at the auction and so now I had my entire crew looking for the three. A couple hours into the shift I got a call from one of the other Gang Detectives. They had found two of the three in a car during a traffic stop and wanted to know if I wanted to stop by and chat with them.

I couldn't get there fast enough. Thankfully nobody recorded what I said to those two in the car. Needless to say I never had any further problems out of those three.

UNWELCOMED CHIROPRACTIC SERVICES

The semi-annual bid board had just happened so there were new faces on the crew. It was always interesting getting to know people and how they react in any given situation. I was on my way to a domestic disturbance with one of the new guys to the crew and I hadn't gone on any calls with him yet. From what I could tell just from watching him he seemed to be extremely quiet; almost too quiet. He always had a scowl on his face and he had a piercing gaze. The call we were going to was down in a trailer park. I have nothing in particular against trailer parks, but there are of course those stereotypes.

We got to the call and could hear yelling and fussing going on inside the trailer. It didn't sound too bad so we decided to knock on the door. The lady of the trailer came to the door and told us that her husband was drunk and breaking furniture because his back hurt. It didn't make much sense to me but whatever. We got the husband to come outside with us and tell us his side of the story. I have to be honest. I wasn't really listening to the guy. He was mainly babbling, yelling, and whining about his back. The longer we let him rant the more worked up he was getting. At some point we came to the decision that the guy was going to jail for breaking up the house.

I was just getting ready to cuff the guy when BOOM! My partner on this call who had yet to say a word planted a forearm shiver in the middle of the guy's chest that knocked him completely off his feet. The guy landed on his back in a heap on the ground outside the trailer. All of the sudden this guy had nothing to say. He was now completely silent. We stood him up and handcuffed him without any problems. About halfway down to Central Headquarters the guy spoke up. All he said was "My back feels better. Thanks."

ONE-GLOVE, THANKS MEDIA

I was working my first six months in the Gang Unit as the intelligence Officer. I was doing general research on gang trends when I came across a story from Asbury Park, New Jersey. It was an article published by that department's intelligence Officer. The focus of the story was a trend being noticed by cops on the street in their city. Apparently gang members had taken to wearing only one glove on their shooting hand to act as a signal to other gang members that they were armed with a gun. I found the information interesting and reached out to the Asbury Park Police Department for permission to use their intelligence in an Officer Safety Bulletin for Omaha.

I wrote the bulletin right before I made the transition to the North Gang Suppression Squad so I was anxious to see if the same one-glove tactic had made its way to Omaha. It wasn't three weeks later when my new partner and I were rolling through a neighborhood controlled by the Small Street Crips. There standing on the corner was three guys. One of whom was wearing a black glove on his right hand; no glove on the left hand. I was excited to put the information to the test.

My partner and I decided not to spook them so we drove past them before circling the block. We decided to jump out on them quick on our next pass. As soon as we came to a stop the banger wearing the single glove took off running. We flanked him as he tried to run around the back side of a house and caught him just after he pitched his gun. The information was accurate, and it was happening in Omaha. Throughout the course of the summer I tracked how many times a gun arrest resulted from an Officer observing a person wearing a single glove. Before long the number of arrests was above twenty. It had become standard procedure to stop and check anybody wearing a single glove. Then the media got involved.

Information put into an original arrest report, called a Uniform Crime Report (U.C.R.) is public knowledge. Information meant to be kept confidential is recorded in a Supplementary report which is only available to cops and attorneys. One day I got lazy and mentioned the one-glove scenario in a U.C.R. I didn't think much of it at the time. Little did I know that reporters and media types have minions that scour every day's reports looking for news stories. A couple of days later I got a call directly from the Gang Lieutenant; which was never good. He asked if I had seen a copy of the current Omaha World Herald newspaper. It turned out one of the newspaper writers had published a story about gang clothing and gang indicators. Prominently featured and quoted was a section from the U.C.R. where I mentioned the one-glove tactic. Almost overnight the one-glove gun arrests ended. The media had successfully taken away a huge police advantage against armed thugs. Thanks a lot media; you made the city a little less safe.

38 MINUTE PURSUIT, BUY A KIA

I know I mentioned it before, but I'm saying it again; police upper-command Officers hate car chases! It all boils down to civil liability and money. When cars get crashed during pursuits the city pays for it. More accurately, the taxpayers pay for it.

I think the year was 2009. The South Gang Suppression Squad was on a stake-out looking for a felony fugitive. They were working on their own radio channel for tactical reasons. Up on the north side we were completely unaware of what the south crew was doing. All of the sudden the police dispatcher put out alert tones for a pursuit in progress. The pursuit was happening on radio channel four so we all switched over to monitor the pursuit. I have to point out at this point in the story that the Sergeant for the south crew was about to retire so he didn't care about getting in trouble for letting a car chase continue. The decision to continue or cancel a vehicle pursuit ultimately fell to the command Officers. After about five minutes it was clear that the Sergeant had no intention of calling off the chase.

Pretty soon every cop in the city was monitoring the chase, hoping to get a piece of the action. The pursuit moved from the southwest precinct into the southeast precinct. I couldn't believe it was still going. Car chases usually end within the first couple of minutes due to cancellation or crashing. Not so with this chase, it was covering the entire city! After about twenty minutes the chase had moved into the northwest precinct. This was quickly becoming legendary. Most chases stay in one precinct. This chase had already been in three.

All of the north gang crew was in the northeast precinct as was usual. None of us thought there was any chance it would reach northeast. There were just too many cops chasing this car, which by the way was a Kia Optima. At about thirty minutes into the chase the south gang Sergeant gave permission over the radio for anybody with a reasonable opportunity to ram the vehicle! The vehicle was on Dodge Street at that point heading eastbound. Maybe it would make it to the northeast precinct after all. About a minute later the Kia jumped onto highway 75 which cuts right through northeast precinct. If you're not directly involved in the chase it's still a lot of fun trying to predict where the suspect vehicle will go next. Two cruisers had already died chasing down the fleeing Kia. Who knew that Kias were so tough? Anyway, my partner and I had now gotten within sight of the Kia which was ever so slowly being corralled by the sheer number of cop cars closing in around it. Just when we thought we had it cornered in a city park it slipped the noose; two more cruisers died in the process. Just before it ended my partner and I came nose to nose with the Kia as it passed us going the opposite direction. About a block later one of the Gang Detectives rammed it during a turn and finally ended the pursuit. All told five cruisers needed to be repaired as the result of the thirty-eight minute car chase. The Kia was still able to be driven onto the tow truck.

As a caveat to this story: The Sergeant did in fact end up in some trouble. Countless cops had to go to internal affairs over the deal. Omaha Police policy stated at the time that only two cruisers were allowed in a car chase. As bad luck would have it one of the news channels had a city cam posted on Dodge Street that showed about twenty cop cars in procession behind the fleeing Kia. It turned into a full-blown upper command witch-hunt for every cruiser that had any part of the chase. Every cruiser with a working camera was audited. Once again my partner and I were spared any punishment because we had the good sense to stay off the radio; that and the fact our car didn't have a camera.

THE RULES OF INTERNAL AFFAIRS

The crusty old cop from the very first story in this book was really a great guy. Not only did he go with me to see my first dead body, he taught me the rules of internal affairs. Some cops had to go to internal affairs so often that jokes were made they had their own chair up there on the sixth floor of Central Headquarters. I was never one of those cops. I stayed away from internal affairs because I didn't break too many important rules, didn't abuse people, and I knew when to keep my mouth shut. The worst part of having to go to internal affairs was the waiting. You always got your "fat packet" A.K.A. formalized citizen complaint a week before you actually had to go to the appointment. That week was always hell. Luckily I had the "Rules of Internal Affairs" to fall back on. Those rules are as follows:

1. ADMIT NOTHING
2. DENY EVERYTHING
3. DEMAND PROOF
4. MAKE COUNTER-ACCUSATIONS

If you think about it those are just pretty solid rules to follow in daily life—especially in relationships! Just kidding; honesty is the best policy unless it means telling on yourself or another cop.

THE SPHINC-TE-LATOR

Drug dealers love to hide drugs in their ass. It's just part of the game. Usually it's just pinched between the cheeks, but when cornered many guys would push it up into their anal cavity. The rule of law regarding the recovery of drugs from the ass region is this: If you can see it, you can grab it. If you can't see the prize, then a lot more work is required. Namely you have to get a search warrant signed by a judge authorizing medical personnel to recover the contraband for you. In order to get the search warrant you have to have pretty darn compelling evidence to articulate your belief to the judge. Sometimes you would actually catch the guy ramming the goods up the chute. Sometimes you could see the drugs on an x-ray. Either way, convincing a judge to give you that warrant is tough and time consuming. There is one other way we found.

I've spoken many times in this book so far about strategy, tactics, and bluffing guys into telling on themselves. Let me tell you the story of the Sphinc-Te-Lator. In those rare times when you had the suspicion that your suspect had pushed the drugs out of sight, a special tool was needed. That tool is called a Sphinc-Te-Lator. In reality it's a mechanics tool used to retrieve small nuts and bolts from engines when your hand won't fit. It's a metal rod with a small grabbing claw on the end of it. The best way to picture it is by thinking of the arcade machine with the claw that grabs the stuffed animals. Put that claw on the end of a straight metal rod and you have the right mental picture.

On occasion the Sphinc-Te-Lator was known to find its way into an interview room during a strip search in progress. More often than not, the mere appearance of the tool on the table was enough to convince all but the most professional and hardened criminal to give up the goods. It's all about the tactics.

ONLY DOGS AND DOLPHINS HEARD THAT

Stress and adrenaline have the most amazing effects on human physiology. Furthermore, everybody reacts differently under extreme stress like the kind you find in police work. This is a story about a dear friend of mine who had the most comical reaction to adrenaline dumps. Under stress my buddy's voice would uncontrollably raise in tone by about three octaves. It wasn't a one-time reaction; it was every time.

It started out as a car chase but quickly turned into a foot chase. It was a notoriously bad guy down in northeast Omaha. My buddy had been the one to initiate the car chase so he was running the show on the ground. Since the suspect was such a bad guy we were taking all the precautions. Setting up the perimeter, calling for the police helicopter, calling for the K-9; everything by the book. When searching for a suspect on the ground you want to work in teams whenever possible for the sake of safety. Plus it's always good to have that witness there if the worst case scenario happens.

Besides having his little voice problem, my buddy also liked to work alone. He went off on his own during the search for the suspect when all of the sudden we all heard the most hideous screech over the radio. It kept repeating over and over the same thing. Nobody was sure what the hell we were hearing. It sounded like a cop in distress so we all got nervous. Finally at long last someone was able to translate the voice on the radio—my buddy was saying "He's in the tree! He's in the tree!"

We were finally able to find the tree in question with the help of the police helicopter and my buddy shining his flashlight in the sky. The suspect had climbed about thirty feet high in some evergreen type tree. The story ended with the suspect in cuffs. One last thing happened. My buddy got punked over the radio by someone saying "Only dogs and dolphins heard that."

GUNS IN THE GRASS

It was about 9:30 at night and we were all headed to Kountze Park for a report of shots-fired. Every cop in the northeast precinct knew the reputation of Kountze Park as a gang infested hole. Uniform Patrol Officers were the first to arrive and quickly had several suspects and a gun in custody. My partner and I along with about a dozen other cops arrived shortly thereafter. Unfortunately for us the media showed up as well. I had no idea how the media arrived so quickly, especially for a routine shots-fired call. No matter, they were there which meant we all had to be on our best behavior.

I always operated on the premise that when there's one gun there's at least one more. So, my partner and I grabbed the rest of the cops and started to make a search line. It was a trick I had learned in the Army; it was ironically termed "doing a police call." Basically everyone gets in a straight line spaced apart about ten feet and walks forward at the same speed. It is a great way to cover a lot of ground when searching for small items; like guns in a city park.

We were just starting our search and almost immediately found two guns just lying in the grass. Unfortunately for our search group a nervous Lieutenant showed up about that time. She was apparently freaked out by the media presence because she ordered everyone to stop what they were doing, get in their cars, and leave. I tried to reason with her but she wasn't having it. So just like that the search team was disbanded. I never could figure out why command Officers always got freaked out by the sight of a news crew. My partner and I stuck around and tried to finish searching the park on our own but we didn't find any more guns. I'm guessing there was at least one more to be found. There was always one more gun to be found.

THANKS FIRE MARSHALL

This is a story of why it was always my practice to have a badge in my wallet when off-duty. I had won a set of four tickets during a radio contest to a concert at the Ranch Bowl. The Ranch Bowl was an iconic place for concerts, but sadly it's gone now. The band playing the concert was called "The Cult." They were hugely popular in the 80's and 90's and were making a comeback in the early 2000's. I was really pumped to see the band up close and personal at such a small venue like the Ranch Bowl.

When I went to pick up my tickets at the radio station I got a voucher for me and three guests, not actual tickets. No matter, as long as we got to see the band! I rounded up my best buddies and we went out partying in advance of the show. By the time we showed up to the venue the line to get in was enormous. We dutifully stood in line and waited with the rest of the concert goers. Finally we made it to the front of the line; and encountered the Fire Marshall. I hadn't noticed that people had started leaving the line in front of us, and now I knew why. The show was completely sold out and the Ranch Bowl had reached maximum capacity. I was devastated. I showed my voucher to the Fire Marshall to no avail. He wouldn't let us in, period. My buddies were looking at me pissed like it was my fault!

Desperate, I did the only thing I could do. I whipped out my badge and asked for a little "professional courtesy." The Fire Marshall looked at me and my badge and I could see him thinking. Finally he stood up and motioned for me and my three buddies to come with him. He walked us around the back of the building and let us in the back door, to the confusion of the huge bouncer standing there. My buddies loved me again. They made a bee-line to the bar; however I had a different plan now. I showed my badge to the bouncer and told him I was going over to the tour bus. He just nodded and didn't give me any grief. I met the tour manager by the door of the tour bus and showed him my badge, hoping I could meet the band. Apparently tour managers and rock stars don't care about badges because I did NOT get to meet the band. Oh well, I got to see the concert and that was good enough. It turned out to be a great show.

PAY PHONE CRACK DISPENSER

At the corner of 42nd and Ames Avenue in Omaha there is a convenience store. It is common knowledge that if you want to buy drugs that is one sure fire place to go. There was always some street level dealer in the parking lot selling weed or crack or whatever else you might want. We used to have the best time stopping the rich White kids from southwest Omaha as they were leaving the parking lot with their just purchased drugs. For the most part we didn't even try and stop the dealers because in a way they were good for our business. Besides, it wouldn't do any good anyway because street level dealers are like cockroaches; as soon as one is gone another one moves in.

Usually the rich kids just wanted to buy weed, which I never found to be a huge crime. I just enjoyed taking it away from them more than anything else. One day however we caught some really rich kids driving a Lexus, and they had bought more than weed. They had stepped it up to crack-cocaine. We cut the kids a break on the crack in exchange for the GOOD description of the dealer that had sold it to them. I know I said we usually didn't bust dealers, but it was the end of the month and our statistics were due to our Sergeant. On the Gang Unit we had to keep stats of our drug seizures. We were down for the month so I figured what the hell.

    The kids gave us a description of the dealer and told us where he had been standing in the lot. We kicked them loose with the warning to never let us see them at that store again. They agreed and headed back west. We went back to the convenience store looking for our prey. We saw our suspect right away; the kids had given us a spot-on description of the guy. We approached him and he was as calm as could be. That was a little odd I thought. If I was holding and selling crack and the cops pulled up I would be a little nervous! Not this guy, he seemed nothing but confident. We patted him down and didn't find anything. I was beginning to think the kids had fooled us. If the crack wasn't on his person then where was it?

I noticed he was standing next to the building when we pulled up so I started checking for any hiding spots nearby. There wasn't anything to be found. We were about to kick the guy loose and cut our losses when I decided to check one more spot. I went over to the pay phone and stuck my finger in the coin return. JACKPOT! There inside the coin return were several small pre-bagged rocks of crack referred to as "twenty-pieces."

We arrested our guy and I put a note in with the arrest packet for the County Attorney's Office. Since we didn't catch the guy with the drugs we needed a little more evidence for a successful prosecution. The County Attorney agreed to hold the guy until we got our hand-swabs back from the lab. The swabs came back positive so we were good. The suspect plead out and we put the fear of God in a couple of kids; justice served.

EXCALIBUR FOOT CHASE

My partner and I were patrolling the area of the 38th Street Bloods. We got behind a car that was full of heads, probably at least six. It was dark so we couldn't be sure. This was exactly what we were looking for, a carload of guys in a known gang area. We had them on a failure to signal a turn and were just getting ready to initiate the traffic stop when the car pulled into a driveway. Before we could pull in behind them the rear door opened up and a guy bailed on foot running hard. My partner was driving so I was the chase Officer. I didn't even wait for the cruiser to stop before I was out the door and after the runner. He had a pretty good lead on me so I was going to have a tough time on this one.

The guy ran down the hill we were on to the end of the block then made a quick left-hand turn. He was temporarily out of my sight, but by the time I made the turn I decided my guy had ran up the alley right next to the street. I was pretty much running blindly hoping I had guessed right when all of the sudden I heard my guy screaming in pain. I followed the sound of the scream and found my guy lying in a crumpled heap on top of a pile of tree limbs. He had unwittingly ran off an embankment and fallen into someone's back yard. I crawled down to him and pulled him free from his tangled mess. He didn't have a gun on him, nor did I find one in the wood pile. That meant he had probably thrown his gun somewhere along the path of the chase.

I had my partner secure him in the cruiser and then I started my search. I didn't give myself very good odds of finding the gun given the over-growth of trees and bushes in the alley. I was just about to give up when my flashlight beam glinted off something metal. There sticking straight up by the barrel out of the dirt was a long barreled revolver. I swear it looked like Excalibur sticking out of the stone. You could throw that gun down a hundred times and not get the same result. It was almost as if he had taken the time to ram it into the ground. I ruled that out because he didn't have that kind of time during the chase. It was just fate I guess.

NEVER LOAN YOUR PHONE

Everybody that worked the Gang Unit or Narcotics Unit got a city phone issued to them. They used to be Nextel's and had a really cool push to talk walkie-talkie feature. They were also pre-loaded with all the important phone numbers you might ever need, including the Chief's phone number. Needless to say they were an item that was considered very sensitive and you never wanted to lose it. Well that's what one of my buddies did.

A shooting had come out one night at a bar on 30th Street. It was a Saturday night so people were everywhere. It quickly turned into a chaotic mess. During the middle of the incident my buddy walked up to me with a look of panic on his face. Panic mixed with anger. He worked the day shift, so at night he worked off-duty at different places. He had been working at a different bar close by when the shooting occurred. In a moment of weakness and bad discretion he had loaned his work phone out to some lady trying to call for a ride. It turned out the lady was certifiably nuts! The minute she had the phone she took off running. My buddy had come to me to help him find the crazy lady...and his phone.

So here we were, stumbling around the area of a nearby shooting looking for a crazy lady with a stolen city phone! Unbelievably we found her walking around aimlessly. But we had a problem; she didn't have the phone. Not only did she not have the phone, she wouldn't say what she had done with it. Quite frankly this lady was so crazy I don't think she knew what she did with the phone! We tried every tactic we could think of: threats, begging, yelling, and reasoning. None of them worked. After an hour we gave up. We tried calling the phone to try and hear it ringing. That didn't work either. Eventually I had to get back to work and he had to go home. Monday morning he had to face the music—it wasn't pretty.

JUST WAITING PATIENTLY

I had just started working with a new partner shortly after making the move to the northeast precinct. It would have been the second year of my career. We worked the Uniform Patrol Bureau so the majority of our time was spent handling 911 calls for service. Through the course of our travels one shift we passed by the intersection of 30th and Ames Avenue about ten times. We were about six hours into our shift when we both looked at each other with a revelation. There had been a car sitting in a Burger King parking lot for our entire shift. This by itself was not strange. It was strange that the same teenage girl had been sitting in the car the entire time.

Normally this would not grab our attention, but for some reason it had. Something didn't seem right. We pulled into the parking lot and made our way up to the car. The girl didn't move as we approached the car. We knocked on her window and she didn't even turn her head. Then I noticed it. I couldn't believe it had taken me so long to see that she had a shotgun propped up on her passenger floorboard.

We slowly and quietly removed her form the car with no problem and put her in handcuffs. I put the shotgun in our trunk after emptying it. We ran a check of this girl and found out that she was recorded in the system with the code A-Adam. This is the police code for a person deemed to be mentally unstable. We took her over to the nearby precinct building so we could talk to her. We asked her the most obvious question; "Why was she sitting in the parking lot all day and night with a loaded shotgun at her feet?" She looked at us with a quizzical look on her face and replied "I was waiting to shoot my boyfriend for cheating on me."

We were able to determine that her boyfriend worked at the Burger King. After talking it over with our Sergeant we chose to involuntarily commit her for a seventy-two hour mental evaluation rather than arrest her. I don't know if her boyfriend ever found out what almost happened to him.

CAREER ENDER

I intentionally saved this story for last. This is the story of the events that spelled the end of my police career. The following is the account of what happened on the night of June 28th, 2010. That was the night I almost died.

We were riding three deep in our Dodge Intrepid, patrolling the area of the 44th Avenue Crips. The area had been really active with gun violence so we were giving it special attention. It was about 9:30 P.M. so darkness had just settled in. We were travelling northbound on 44th Avenue going up a long hill towards Spaulding Street. From a block out we could see five guys standing at the mouth of an alley by a driveway. Per our M.O. our plan was to come in hot and jump out; if somebody ran so much the better.

As we got closer we could see the guy in the back of the group was starting to "fade." All three of us in the cruiser had clued into the guy fading so I told my partners to "get ready!" I was sitting in the back seat and started to open the door to get a good jump in the event the guy in the back did start running. We came screeching to a stop and I bailed out of the back seat passenger door of our cruiser at a half run. The guy we had been focused on took two or three steps like he was going to run and then turned and emptied a revolver at me. It was surreal. All my senses had turned on me. I could barely hear the gunshots, but I could certainly see the muzzle flashes. I froze temporarily and was on full sensory overload.

I had plenty of experience with adrenaline dumps; in fact the last five years on the Gang Unit had been one adrenaline dump after the next. I thought I was immune to its effects by now. After all the successful foot chases with armed gangbangers I had developed a false sense of invincibility. It all came crashing down on my head.

As soon as the shooter's gun had run dry he started running down the alley. I was getting my wits back and started doing damage control. The first thing I did was pat myself down for the feel of blood. I honestly didn't know if I'd been hit or not. My scalp was on fire and felt like it was trying to crawl off my skull. Time was all distorted. I decided I hadn't been hit, but by now it was too late to shoot back. I got on the radio and yelled "shots-fired at police!" The shooter was now out of sight down the alley and I was faced with a critical decision: Stay and sort out the mess or chase blindly after the guy that just tried to kill me! I decided to stay put. After all, I didn't know where my partners were and what their status was. For all I knew one of them had been shot.

I turned to look back at the cruiser and saw that they were "88." It was time to get re-focused. There were three guys that had voluntarily hit the ground when their buddy started shooting, while the fourth had run into the nearby house. I had thought very seriously about shooting that fourth guy. My partners and I moved in on the three on the ground. My partners searched and cuffed the three on the ground while I watched the house in the event that fourth guy decided to start shooting. The police radio had put out a "Help an Officer" status so we could hear the sounds of every cop in the city coming to back us up. The sound of all those sirens was strangely comforting.

As I sat there watching the house I put out the best description I could of the shooter. It wasn't very good because my vision had tunneled in on the muzzle flashes of his gun. My hope was that a responding Officer would stumble across a guy running down the street while on the way to the scene.

One by one Officers started showing up from all directions. The first command Officer on the scene was the northeast precinct Lieutenant. He kept asking me if I was okay. By now my senses were back under control and I was in a state of rage. I wanted more than anything to start looking for the shooter, but I knew there were more pressing issues. The guy that had run into the house now made it a barricade situation. That meant the S.W.A.T. team would have to be called out.

The hour and a half it took for the S.W.A.T. team to arrive seemed to go by in about ten minutes. Maybe I wasn't as okay as I was telling everyone, and myself. The three suspects that hit the ground were already transported to Central Headquarters, so at that point I was relegated to the role of bystander. All around the surrounding neighborhood, cops were checking anybody and everybody that remotely fit the description of the shooter. It appeared he had gotten away clean. He was probably already in a house laughing and hiding the gun.

The S.W.A.T. team was successful in getting the fourth guy to surrender and come out of the house. He too was transported to Central. At last the situation was "88" and we were able to start searching the yard and the house. We found another gun hidden outside the house in the BBQ grill along with a big bag of ecstasy pills. Just inside the front door to the house was a loaded shotgun. Another gun was found hidden upstairs somewhere. By this point the adrenaline was wearing off and I was now exhausted. It was now time to start the rest of the investigation.

None of the four guys that we caught would give up the name of the shooter. I guess I could respect that in a sick way. I went back to the scene the very next day at the beginning of my shift. It was like a ghost town. None of the usual bangers were anywhere to be found. I went and stood at the exact spot where I had been when the shooting started. There in the door molding of a parked car was a gouge where one of the bullets had impacted. I guessed it had been about a foot from hitting me in the upper chest, or possibly the head. I have no idea where the other rounds landed or how close they had come to hitting me. I guess it didn't matter. I had survived and that was what mattered.

EPILOGUE

I continued to work on the Gang Unit for several months after the night I was shot at, but I was a changed man. The changes were not for the better. Five long years on the Gang Unit had taken their toll on my mind. It continued to eat at me that the shooter was never caught or even identified. My behavior became more and more erratic. I was fighting with co-workers, kicking in car doors of gangbangers, and generally felt like I was losing my mind. I wasn't losing my mind. I was suffering from Post Traumatic Stress Disorder.

Eventually I asked to leave the Gang Unit and was transferred to a spot on the Major Crimes Unit within the Criminal Investigations Bureau. I never could resolve all the emotions I still had every time I put on the gun-belt. My work started to suffer and I began to take a lot of sick time; I had never used my sick time previously. I had never wanted to miss a day of police work. I loved it too much to ever miss a shift.

One day at work I got up from my desk and walked into my Lieutenant's office. I told him I was unfit for duty. The next stop was the Captain's office. I was placed on administrative leave pending a fit-for-duty evaluation. In the meantime I visited the offices of the Police Union Attorney and told him my intentions to file for a service connected disability due to P.T.S.D.

All the paperwork was filed and on November 17th, 2011 I was officially retired. If you're reading this I want to thank you for staying to the end. My career was a great ride, one I will never forget. I hope you enjoyed re-living these memories with me— GOD BLESS! Ryan Sedlacek #1624, Retired.

Made in the USA
San Bernardino, CA
21 January 2017